61/1081

CW01044358

50

MEMORIES OF THE BRITISH RAJ
A SOLDIER IN INDIA

By the same author

SELF-HELP PHYSIOTHERAPY—*Faber & Faber*

MEMORIES
OF
THE BRITISH RAJ

A Soldier In India

BRIGADIER R.C.B. BRISTOW O.B.E.

JOHNSON

LONDON

First Published 1974

ISBN 0 85307 132 2

Printed and made by
Clarke, Doble & Brendon Ltd.
Plymouth

FOREWORD

by

GENERAL SIR ROB LOCKHART, K.C.B., C.I.E., M.C.
Commander-in-Chief Indian Army,
15 August–31 December 1947

Much has been written about the Partition of India in 1947 and about the tragic events that occurred at that time; but this book is, I believe, the first to contain an account of some of these events by a British officer who actually served with troops dealing with the widespread and violent disorder which took place in the Punjab that year.

Brigadier Bristow was a regular officer of the Indian Army. After an interesting account of his early days as a cadet, and then as an officer in his Indian Regiment between the two World Wars and during the Second World War, he devotes the second part of his book to the tasks confronting the Army in the Punjab in 1947 and how they were carried out.

These tasks were complex and unpleasant. The Army had to try to protect all who were in danger of loss of life or property; to rescue refugees, to safeguard communications and important installations; and to restore law and order. All this had to be done at a time when the civil and military administrations of the two new Dominions were undergoing reorganisation necessitated by Partition. Public servants of every grade—policemen, railway personnel, post office workers—were on the move: Hindus and Sikhs leaving Pakistan for India, and Muslims leaving India for Pakistan. There were thousands of refugees fleeing in both directions from one country to the other.

Brigadier Bristow makes it clear that there were some instances of troops allowing their religious feelings to influence their actions, but that the majority of the Indian Army units did their duty splendidly I know well. I believe that the discipline and devotion to duty of the Indian soldiers, still mostly under the command of their British officers, prevented even greater disasters than those that occurred.

Brigadier Bristow believes that had Partition been deferred until, say, April 1948 the tragedy in the Punjab would not have occurred. It is true that many officers who served in India, including myself, would have agreed with him. Had officials of every grade in the civil services, and all the personnel of the armed services, been in position in their respective new countries before Independence Day, it seems there would have been a better chance of preventing widespread disorder.

On the other hand there are many, including some best qualified to know, who consider that to have deferred the grant of Independence to a later date would have resulted in even greater disasters and many more casualties than actually occurred.

I enjoyed reading this book and consider it a valuable contribution to the history of India and to that of the Indian Army. I hope it will be widely read.

R. M. M. LOCKHART

CONTENTS

To

*The Dogras, the British Officers of
the Punjab Boundary Force 1947, and Elsa, my wife,
who also wore the King's uniform.*

ILLUSTRATIONS

MAPS

INTRODUCTION

Book I describes life in the old Indian Army of British officers and Indian soldiers, both in peace and war, from 1918 until the independence of India and Pakistan in 1947.

During the Raj the martial classes who composed the Indian Army were among the most loyal friends of the British, probably because there are few closer ties than those made by serving in the same regiment, or sharing a trench or a bivouac. Although I have mentioned several of the martial classes, I have attempted to describe in detail the history and character of only one group, the Dogras, pronounced Dohgras, with whom I spent most of my service. The history of the Dogras explains their ancient feud with the Muslims in the struggle for power and territory in the Punjab, which broke out anew in 1947 when British influence ended.

Book II gives an account of the Communal War which followed independence, and deals particularly with the life saving operations of an Indian Infantry Brigade, with a few British officers, during appalling massacres in the Punjab.

Most of the key figures who planned the transfer of power in India and Pakistan have endeavoured to justify their policies in their autobiographies or through their biographers. But the wisdom of those policies can only be judged objectively when persons at the receiving end, such as myself, record their experiences in trying to put them into effect.

As a Brigade Commander during the Communal War my responsibility was confined to a relatively small area, and so the conclusions I reach at the end of the book may be regarded as parochial. Nevertheless, consideration should be given to the views not only of those high in authority, but also of those on the spot and nearer events.

Unfortunately there is a lack of eye-witness records by those who were present during the massacres in the Punjab. As historians cannot make fair judgments if secrets of the past remain untold, I have tried to add my own evidence before it is too late. My account is also a tribute to members of the British rearguard, who have received little credit for saving many thousands of lives.

India Office Library and Records, London, were able to supply few details concerning the Punjab conflict, but I am very grateful to the staff for their courtesy and help in providing other information. The regimental histories of the old Indian Army end at the time of independence, and therefore contain little about the communal war that followed. To verify facts I have had to rely mainly on brother officers present at the time, who have helped generously. Their experience and views have greatly influenced the conclusions I have expressed.

Particularly I thank the following. Appointments shown were those held in 1947.

Mr. I. E. Jones, C.I.E, Commissioner Jullundur Civil Division; Mr. D. Gainsford, C.I.E., Deputy Inspector General Police Jullundur Civil Division; Major General B. W. Key, C.B., D.S.O., M.C., Commander Lahore Area Pakistan; Brigadier J. B. Keenan, Commander 43rd Lorried Infantry Brigade, later Liaison Officer between East Punjab Area and Lahore Area; Lt.-Colonel P. S. Mitcheson, D.S.O., O.B.E., General Staff Officer 1, East Punjab Area India; Lt.-Colonel J. L'A. Bell, M.B.E., Commander 3rd Royal Bn. Frontier Force Regiment; Lt.-Colonel C. J. Boulter, M.C., O.B.E., Commander 3rd (Para) Bn. 1st Punjab Regiment; Major P. M. C. Hussey, Central India Horse; Major E. C. Gleeson, 2nd Bn. Dogra Regiment; Major D. H. Donovan, M.C., 1st Bn. 9th Gurkha Rifles; Major D. H. Jones, Brigade Major, 11th Indian Infantry Brigade; Major C. H. Williams, Staff Officer 11th Indian Infantry Brigade.

I am grateful to Mr. W. A. Barnes, late Principal, Government College Lyallpur, Punjab, for checking the manuscript.

His intimate knowledge of the Punjab has been most helpful.

I thank the Dowager Countess Wavell for kind permission to quote from Field Marshal Earl Wavell's Foreword to *Fourth Indian Division*.

R. C. B. BRISTOW

BOOK ONE

1918-46

Life in the Old Indian Army in Peace and War

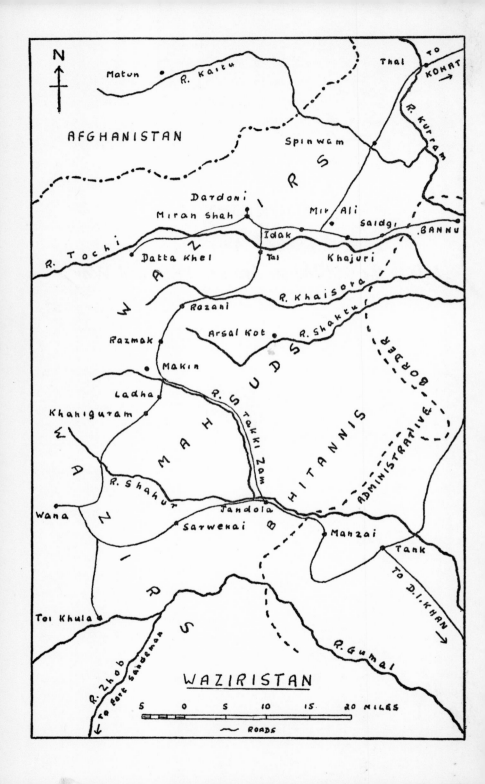

WAZIRISTAN

CHAPTER I

RETURN TO INDIA

In 1918 the First World War was in its last year. Like my father, Major Robert Bristow, I had decided to be a regular soldier, and was studying in the small Army Class at King's College School, Wimbledon, for the army entrance examination for regular commissions. In April, thanks to my tutors, I was successful in my first attempt.

Throughout the war my father held an administrative appointment in France, as owing to an injury and age he was no longer fit for active operations, and we saw him briefly only once a year. During the four war years my mother Maud courageously looked after her children alone; the others were my younger brother Basil and sister Una the youngest. Our home was in New Malden, Surrey, then surrounded by green fields and known locally as The Village, but now grown into a large London suburb.

Air raids on London occasionally brought the war closer. During air alarms the family took shelter under the stairs, but as an embryo regular soldier, I did not consider that in keeping with my future profession, and equipped with an old steel helmet and binoculars given me by Ralph Eales kept watch in the garden. Ralph, my mother's youngest brother was a field artillery officer in France, spent his short leaves with us and was our wartime hero.

My air observer role worried my mother, but gave comfort to the younger children who felt safe so long as the sentry did not report aircraft overhead. Occasionally I spotted aircraft flying high, but even if hostile the danger to Malden was slight, as their target was London. Nevertheless the alarm sirens drove all to cover and disrupted life.

B

Having served in Egypt, South Africa, Somaliland, India and France, my father had wide experience overseas, and advised me to join the British Army, for in India he saw the red light for Britons, and forecast the end of the Raj before I should complete my career. While respecting his kindly advice I was attracted to the land of my birth, having entered this world in the North-West Frontier Province in 1900, and had a strong desire to serve in the Indian Army. My father generously accepted my wish provided I applied to join a Gurkha regiment, for in India to him Gurkhas were the nearest approach to British soldiers. Before taking the entrance examination I therefore gave the Indian Army as my first preference. When the results appeared showing that I had been accepted I was delighted.

War casualties created an urgent need for young officers, who were useless in the Indian Army until they could speak the language of their men. In peace time Indian Army cadets went to the Royal Military College, Sandhurst, for eighteen months, and then were attached to a British battalion in India for a year, during which they studied Urdu. As war demands could be met only by reducing that period drastically, cadets joined an Officer Cadet Battalion in England for three months, and then a Cadet College in India for six months, either at Quetta or Wellington. By studying Urdu at the college they were fit to go straight to an Indian unit on being commissioned.

The group I joined carried out preliminary training with an Officer Cadet Battalion at Catterick in Yorkshire. Chosen from men who had shown courage and leadership on the battlefield, the other cadets of the battalion were the pick of the British and Dominion armies, many with decorations for bravery. Two companies of British cadets, and one company of Dominion cadets, were composed of men in their middle twenties, whereas in contrast with those veterans, the Indian Army cadets comprising the fourth company were mostly straight from school. We were still in Britain among familiar sights and people, but were soon to sail for a very different world.

Prior to departure for India we enjoyed a few weeks' leave, which passed all too quickly, and in September I said good-bye to my mother, brother and sister; my father was still in France.

Basil, five years younger than myself, was left with a damaged heart after rheumatic fever, and died when fifteen. His loss was a deep sorrow to the family. Una was determined to follow her father and brother into the army, qualified as a nurse at Guy's Hospital, London, and joined Queen Alexandra's Imperial Military Nursing Service. She married an army doctor, Captain (later Brigadier) Charles Marsden, R.A.M.C., and so, like her mother, spent many years within sound of the bugles.

On the journey to India our first adventure was several days in a troop train crossing France to Marseilles, from where we sailed to Karachi. In the Mediterranean a few submarine scares occurred, but escorting Japanese destroyers saw us safely through to Port Said. Regarding the Japanese as staunch allies, I little imagined that in days to come I should be engaged in a bitter war against them. The train journey across the Sind Desert was hot and dusty, but when we climbed into the mountains, Quetta was pleasantly cool at an altitude of 5,600 feet. The scene was very different from green England, as except for limited areas of cultivation, the Quetta plateau was arid and surrounded by bare rocky moutains, with the predominant colour grey-brown like our khaki uniform.

Whereas at Catterick, in a hutted camp, our accommodation was similar to that of other ranks, here it was intended for officers, as the Cadet College occupied the premises of the Staff College, which had closed down for the duration of the war. Four cadets occupied a comfortable bungalow, in which each had a separate bedroom and bathroom, thus ensuring privacy and a quiet study for work. The public rooms were comfortably furnished and included a good library.

The instructional staff were carefully chosen British officers of the Indian Army, and sergeant instructors of the British Army, who created a happy atmosphere, and strove to turn us into good subalterns. My platoon commander was Captain (later Lt.-Colonel) Gordon Borrowman of the 4th P.W.O. Gurkha Rifles. Our friendship continued after Quetta, and included our wives when he married Gem McLeod, and I married Elsa Fairfax. He was a fine artist whose sketches were famous in India; some of his portraits of Indian Army soldiers, especially of his beloved Gurkhas, hang in the National Army Museum.

For six months our lives revolved around the parade ground, weapon ranges, riding school, lecture halls, the *munshi*, games, competitions and examinations, all of which I enjoyed except the last. To learn Urdu, the common language of the Indian Army, we were grouped in small classes under a *munshi* (Indian teacher). Pure Urdu was spoken in the United Provinces, and related dialects in adjacent areas, but in distant provinces quite different languages existed. In order that men from different parts could work together a common army language was necessary. For most cadets progress in learning Urdu was slow until they joined their regiments, and had to communicate and work by using the vernacular.

At games I played for the first eleven hockey team, but my favourite sport was riding. There was keen competition to get into No. 1 Ride, for its members enjoyed the privilege of hunting with the Quetta Hounds. We were trained by British sergeant riding instructors from the Cavalry and Royal Artillery, whose methods were tough and humour in keeping. When jumping, a favourite command was, 'Cross stirrups, knot reins, fold arms'. Some of the meaner old troop horses knew the order well, and seized the opportunity to get rid of the weight on their backs, by a sudden hesitation or swerve before a jump.

On one of those occasions a cadet in my ride became unseated, and was hanging on perilously, with his arms around his horse's neck, and one foot over its back. He was making a brave attempt to return to the saddle, when the harsh voice of the instructor yelled, 'Mr. . . . why don't you fall off like a gentleman, sir, instead of hanging on like a blasted monkey?' The disheartened acrobat gave up and rolled in the dust. We had many good laughs in the riding school, and in turn all provided the cause. What a lot the modern army must miss without the horse.

The best riders were gradually grouped in No. 1 Ride, and I

was fortunate to be chosen. About half way through the course the Chief Riding Instructor, Lt.-Colonel Naylor, gave No. 1 Ride a severe cross-country test to prove our fitness to hunt, and after he was satisfied, briefed us on the strict code of riding to hounds. Parading for the hunt, and trotting off to the meet, was always a happy occasion.

The field was composed mainly of officers of the Quetta garrison together with some of the wives. The hounds were thoroughbred English foxhounds, and their quarry jackal, which is bigger and stronger than a fox. Much of the country over which we galloped was hard and stony, and the worst obstacles were water channels at the bottom of deep nullahs, which entailed sliding down a precipitous slope, a standing leap over the water, or into it, and a clamber up the other side. On one hunt we galloped twelve miles, and ended with one jackal, one hound, one whip and two officer cadets, of whom I was one; all the others had fallen by the way. By then we were starting to climb the hills on the edge of the Quetta plateau, with the hound on the tail of the jackal which occasionally turned its head to snarl. The hound was either too tired or too frightened to close, and when the jackal disappeared over the brow of a ridge the whip called off the dog, which looked most relieved. That jackal deserved to live, though it was probably back at night looking for somebody's chickens.

The only event in which I distinguished myself at Quetta was the mounted and dismounted weapon's competition; the weapons being rifle, revolver, light automatic, sword and lance. I was placed second to Fred Daw, a veteran of the Australian Army. Several members of the Dominion forces were given cadetships at the college, and most of them were Australians. In the competition I came first in the mounted tent-pegging with a lance, and first in the mounted sword-versus-sword, in which the riders wore a leather jacket, and a face and head guard surmounted by a wood and paper plume. Two riders with wooden swords opposed each other, and the winner was the first to cut off his opponent's plume. I got through several rounds just because the opposing horse would not face a brandished sword, and gave its

rider little chance. From the hunters in No. 1 Ride I had discovered a wonderful charger, and kept the secret very much to
myself, as the grab for good horses was ruthless. He never failed
to leap past the opposing horse close enough to give me an easy
cut at my adversary's plume, and far from being frightened
seemed to enjoy the game.

The last stage of the competition was to clear six jumps, after
each one stab a dummy with a sword, and then dismount and
knock down six falling-plates with a revolver. On arriving at
the plates I was ahead on points, but shot badly and dropped
to second place.

At the end of the final competitions and of the verbal and
written examinations we awaited our fate. Meanwhile we were
instructed to apply for three regiments in order of preference,
helped by a booklet describing the classes recruited in the Indian
Army, and the class composition of each regiment. Enthusiastic-
ally I perused the booklet in which all classes and regiments were
described in proud terms. With envy I scanned the cavalry regiments, considering life ideal in a world of horses and polo, but,
without private means, out of the question; however, I discovered
that the officers of two Gurkha regiments did play polo. Though
most Gurkha stations were high in the hills with no facilities for
polo, the 2nd and 9th had their home on the plains at Dehra
Dun, where polo was played. As first choice I applied for the
9th Gurkha Rifles.

Competition was always keen for the popular Gurkhas, and
vacancies difficult to get. Apart from a family connection, which
I did not possess, the only hope was to pass out higher than my
rivals. To my relief I had graduated 19th out of 150, been commissioned into His Majesty's Land Forces as a 2nd Lieutenant,
with effect from 15 April 1919, and attached to the 2nd Battalion 9th Gurkha Rifles at Dehra Dun; permanent postings
were not being made until the wartime army had been reduced
to peace establishment. I bought myself a black star for each
shoulder, as worn by rifle regiments, which I considered more
distinguished than the general pattern of gilt star.

The 9th Gurkha Rifles, raised in 1817, had a fine record and proud traditions, and even with my slight experience I recognised a good regiment. The 2nd Battalion had recently returned from Mesopotamia, after two and a half years' active service; most of the officers and men were on leave, and present were only a few officers headed by Major H. Mullaly. Within a year Herbert Mullaly died from pneumonia, during operations in Waziristan, a sad loss to the regiment. Their medals and decorations marked the officers as veterans of the First World War, in which the regiment had won twelve battle honours in France and Mesopotamia. I was aware of a wide experience gap between the others and myself, very different from life in Quetta where we were all beginners.

To the Gurkhas, who were not Indians but Nepalese, I took an immediate liking. Short in stature, strongly built, with semi-Mongolian features, they were quick to smile or laugh. They loved being soldiers, and if discipline means cheerful obedience of orders, no soldier possesses this quality more than a Gurkha. I was very disappointed at first that I could not communicate with them intelligently, for neither could they understand my smattering of Urdu, nor I their Gurkhali. Because of the difficulty of teaching Urdu to Gurkhas, they were an exception in being permitted to use their own language. As a matter of urgency I engaged a *munshi* to teach me.

The battalion was organised with a headquarters and four companies. In headquarters were four British Officers and four Viceroy's Commissioned Officers (V.C.O.s). The latter held the ranks of Subedar-Major, Subedar and Jemadar, and corresponded roughly to Warrant Officers in the British Army, with the additional honour of being saluted by the men. At the top were the Commanding Officer, and his deputy the Second-in-Command. The Subedar-Major was adviser to the C.O. on personal matters concerning the Gurkhas, and, as the senior V.C.O., held in great respect. Battalion staff work was divided between the Adjutant and the Quartermaster, each assisted by a V.C.O., the Jemadar Adjutant and the Jemadar Quartermaster. The fourth V.C.O. was the Signal Jemadar.

Each of the four companies had two British Officers—the

Company Commander and Company Officer. Thus a battalion required twelve British Officers, but about six more were included on its list, as roughly this number were absent on staff and other appointments. During the summer leave season, with many absent, even a junior subaltern often found himself in temporary command of a company, which consisted of three platoons, each of 35 men commanded by a V.C.O. Later there were changes in organisation, with the addition of specialist officers in headquarters.

In Gurkha regiments, before independence, the King's Commissioned Officers remained British, but in the rest of the Indian Army, after the First World War, Indians were given similar commissions in increasing proportion. At first in small numbers they went to Sandhurst and Woolwich, and when commissioned were called King's Indian Commissioned Officers (K.I.C.O.s). To increase the number in 1932, the Indian Military Academy was established in Dehra Dun, and those commissioned from there were called Indian Commissioned Officers (I.C.O.s). Thus there were three classes of commissioned officers—the British known as B.O.s—Indian of equivalent status known as I.C.O.s (including the early K.I.C.O.s)—V.C.O.s already described, of junior status.

Between the two great wars the I.C.O.s were posted only to certain selected units, which were gradually to become completely Indianised. The Second World War began with about 3,000 B.O.s and 500 I.C.O.s, but segregation of I.C.O.s in certain units ceased, and they were integrated throughout the army except in Gurkha regiments. I did not serve in a battalion with I.C.O.s until 1938, and so for many years worked only with B.O.s and V.C.O.s.

Soon after I joined the 2/9th my company commander went on a course, leaving me temporarily in command, and I found it stimulating to have responsibility for the first time. The training at Quetta helped with my duties, but much could be learned only from experience, and the advice of the Subedar, or senior V.C.O. of the company. As the hot summer season had begun, training was confined mostly to the parade ground and firing ranges, and took place in the early morning and late afternoon. Office work was done before lunch.

Games in the evening provided the main recreation, when the men played football and basket ball, and young officers were expected to take part or referee. Tennis, squash and golf were available at the officers' club, but my passion at that time was riding, with an eye to polo. I was surprised and disappointed to discover that it would cost more to play polo in infantry, than in Indian cavalry.

In cavalary an officer received an allowance to maintain two horses. Troop horses in Indian cavalry, in height from about 14·2 to 15·1 hands, were small enough for polo, and those suitable were chosen and trained as polo ponies. In addition to any private ponies a cavalry officer possessed, he could augment his string with troop horses, by paying a modest insurance charge to Government. With troop horses it was even possible to mount some V.C.O.s in stations where players were scarce. When playing in tournaments all trained troop horses were pooled, and the best allotted to the team. In the cavalry cheap horses made polo available even for the poor, but they did not exist in the infantry. However, as a start, I was determined to acquire one pony, and to be content with two chukkas, though most riders played four or six; two eight minute chukkas were the limit for one pony.

A beginner is helped by playing on a trained pony, but such an animal was beyond my slender resources, and I therefore decided to acquire a young animal and train it myself. The best were well-bred imported Australian ponies, but even these were too expensive, and I had to settle for a six-year-old country-bred stallion, which turned out a great disappointment.

Before being mixed with other ponies he had to be gelded, which operation seemed to add deep resentment to his bad temper, probably arising from generations of harsh treatment. I did all possible to win his affection and improve his temper, but kindness and rewarding lumps of sugar had little effect. Because of his hard and unbending character I called him Flint. Strictly according to a text book and with much enthusiasm I marked out a riding school, began his training, and gradually introduced him to a polo stick and ball; but he always hated the sight of them.

Slow progress was being made with the *munshi* and Flint, the reluctant polo pony, when, in the middle of May, the battalion was ordered to mobilise for a move to the frontier. The Afghans had invaded India, to begin the 3rd Afghan War, and we were sent to Kohat, the forward base for operations in the Kurram valley. Events preceding the war, and closely connected with it, had seriously disturbed the peace in India.

In February 1919, Amir Habibullah Khan was murdered, and succeeded by his third son Amanullah Khan. During the First World War Habibullah had kept Afghanistan neutral, despite strong pressure by the Turks, a War Party of Afghans, and Indian revolutionaries conspiring in Kabul. With other aspirants to the throne, and suspected of complicity in the murder, the new Amir was not acceptable to all his subjects as an absolute monarch. There arose a typical mediaeval situation, in which an insecure king sought to strengthen his position by a successful war; if he could regain the North-West Frontier Province lost in 1820 to the Sikhs, his throne would be safe.

The British were exhausted after the First World War, in which the Empire had suffered a million killed. The British and Indian armies were in process of demobilisation and reconstitution, with many troops still overseas. In India the authorities were fully occupied with unrest and insurrection, especially in the Punjab. That took the usual form of rioting, murder, arson and the destruction of government property, such as police stations, post offices and the railway. With hardly enough troops in India to deal with internal security, war with Afghanistan was most undesirable. Amanullah and the War Party were encouraged by mounting insurrection in India, and by the assurance of Indian revolutionaries in Kabul that massive support awaited the Afghans in India, with insurgents tying down the Indian forces.

The climax of the insurrection was the unfortunate shooting at Amritsar on 13 April 1919. Following two days of violent rioting, arson and the murder of isolated Britons, a vast mob, defying a stern ban, assembled at Jallianwala Bagh, a walled space inside the congested city. Brigadier-General Dyer with fifty Gurkha and Indian soldiers with rifles, and forty Gurkhas armed only with *kukris* (knives) entered the Bagh which had few exits.

In a confined space, the troops were hemmed in by a hostile mob of several thousands, the nearest of them within eight or nine yards, and by a sudden rush the soldiers could have been overwhelmed. Dyer ordered his men to fire, killing 379 and wounding about 1,200. The isolation of the small party of troops, and the dangerous proximity of the mob, probably had some influence on the extent of the firing.

Dyer believed that he was dealing not merely with riots but with insurrection, or war against the Crown, which, as the use of minimum force had so far failed, could be put down only by strong action. The shooting immediately ended the insurrection. That helped the army to reinforce the frontier against the Afghans and to end quickly a war, which otherwise might have spread, lasted a long time, and cost thousands of lives. Dyer was among those sent to the frontier where he played a notable part. Although the Amritsar shooting helped to restore peace, the Hunter Parliamentary Committee of Enquiry condemned Dyer for not using minimum force; and he was relieved of his command. Twenty-eight years later the Punjab was ablaze, I held the same position as Dyer—Commander Jullundur Brigade—and like him had to face the mob.

Whereas a soldier does not hesitate to shoot in war, he hates no duty more than shooting at fellow citizens, even when these are rioting. As normally the rioters cannot shoot back, to the soldier his own action seems cowardly. However a government has a duty to stop arson, looting and murder, and, as a last resort, minimum shooting was considered justified. The terrible cost of evading this duty was shown in 1947, when the new governments of India and Pakistan failed to act against murderous mobs, and half a million people, including small children, were slaughtered cowering behind the doors of their homes. In those terrible killings and atrocities Amritsar was again in the lead.

From the Jallianwala Bagh tragedy lessons were learnt both by the Government and the rebels. Whereas communal fights and riots recurred periodically, anti-government agitation tended to take the form of Mahatma Gandhi's non-violent non-co-operation; a way of defying law and authority with the advantage of not risking lives. The Government was determined to prevent a repetition of the Bagh, and so a strict drill was laid down for troops called out in aid of the civil power, to ensure that they would use only minimum force, and not be carried away by the heat of the moment. Briefly the procedure and drill were as follows.

Responsibility for calling out troops rested with the civil authority. If the police were unable to control a rioting mob, threatening life and property, a magistrate would ask the officer commanding the troops on the spot to disperse them, which he confirmed in writing by signing a form. If possible, the troops would run out concertina barbed wire to their front so as to avoid a hand-to-hand encounter. A red banner was unfurled between two poles warning the mob to disperse, or else the troops would fire. Attention was drawn by the sounding of a bugle, and the warning repeated several times through a megaphone by the magistrate. If the mob still refused to withdraw, the officer had the duty to disperse them by using minimum force.

Warnings were seldom ignored, but if they were the officer would normally order one man to fire one round at the ring-leader. If that failed to disperse the mob, fire would gradually be increased by a few rounds at a time, and stopped immediately the mob showed signs of moving away. Empty cartridge cases would be collected and counted to prove the use of minimum force, for a court of enquiry would certainly follow. As soon as possible the wounded had to be given first aid and taken to hospital. In the absence of a magistrate, troops could use force only in self-defence or to defend the lives of other citizens.

Following introduction of the drill, shooting incidents became rare, and although we often practised the drill I was not present during civil disturbances until after independence in 1947. Events then are described in later chapters.

In 1919, had the insurrection been allowed to spread, and to continue into May, it would have coincided with the Afghan invasion, tied down troops, and obstructed communications to the frontier. Fortunately it was put down before the invasion. Without the help of the insurgents in India it was even more important for Amanullah to raise all the frontier tribes in a *jehad* (holy war), and so cause wide dispersion of British forces. To do this the Afghans endeavoured to rouse the Pathans to action from Chitral to Baluchistan, and to encourage them crossed the frontier at several places. The full support of the tribes was likely only if Amanullah achieved a spectacular initial success, which he hoped to attain with his two main attacks against the Khyber Pass and the Kurram Valley.

West of the Khyber the Afghans crossed the frontier on 4 May, and occupied the village of Bagh, hoping to join forces with the Mohmands to the north and Afridis to the south, but the help of the tribesmen did not extend beyond harassing British communications. Landi Kotal, the forward British post, was garrisoned only by frontier militia, who were weakened by the desertion of their Afridis. Regular reinforcements were rushed up to Landi Kotal, retook Bagh on 11 May, then crossed the frontier and occupied Dakka on 17 May.

The northern attack had ended in rapid defeat. Afghan prestige suffered a further blow on 27 May, when the British stormed and took the large Afghan fort of Spin Baldak on the Baluchistan front. To impress the tribes Amanullah's only hope now rested with General Nadir Khan, who had concentrated in the province of Khost two cavalry regiments, fourteen battalions and forty-eight guns.

Part of that force was detached to attack British posts in the Upper Kurram valley. With the main body Nadir Khan left Matun on 23 May, and advanced down the Kaitu valley; a clever strategic approach, taking advantage of the Khost salient into India. With no opposition he reached Spinwam, from where he could turn north and cut off the Upper Kurram, or turn

south and cut off the Upper Tochi. Had he chosen the Tochi and
seized Idak, all Waziristan would have rallied to him. By moving away from Waziristan and towards Thal, he lost the close
support of thousands of Wazir and Mahsud tribesmen, who,
without a supply system, could not fight far from their own
territory.

Thal was defended by only four Indian battalions, four mountain guns and a squadron of cavalry. The Afghans approached on
27 May, accompanied by several thousand tribesmen. Occupying
all the surrounding hills, for four days Nadir Khan shelled Thal
and made nibbling attacks, dilatory tactics which lost him the
great advantage of strategic surprise. With considerable
superiority in numbers and artillery, had he made a concerted
attack Thal might have fallen.

The 45th Brigade, under Brigadier-General Dyer, advanced
from Kohat to relieve Thal with four battalions, including one
British, the 1/25th London Regiment (T.A.), and made contact
with the Afghans on 1 June. Despite intense heat, the relief
column, together with the beleagured garrison, attacked resolutely
for two days, and on the third day the Afghans began a disorderly
retreat up the Kurram valley; they could not reach Afghanistan
quickly enough. The invasion was over, an armistice declared,
and on 8 August a peace treaty signed.

The failure of the Afghans had a sobering effect on them, and
as a result the British enjoyed peaceful relations with Afghanistan during the last 28 years of the Raj. The tribesmen were
bitterly disappointed at the weak performance of the Afghans,
and parts of the frontier remained unsettled, especially Waziristan, where the Wazirs and Mahsuds refused to make peace.

Dyer was acclaimed for his decisive victory, but then had to
face the Hunter Committee, whose verdict on the tragedy at
Amritsar deprived him of a promising future. Obviously the role
of soldier had suited him better than that of policeman.

The 2/9th Gurkhas arrived in Kohat on 31 May to join the
16th Indian Division under Major-General Sir William Beynon.
As the 3/9th Gurkhas were in Thal the 2nd Battalion had a
personal interest in the relief. The 45th Brigade had just left to

relieve Thal, and expecting to follow, we were very surprised when Dyer defeated the Afghans in two days, and disappointed at not taking an active part.

On arrival at Kohat I was full of military ardour, but my hope to see action for the first time was not realised. The battalion was ordered to provide a cipher officer at Divisional Headquarters, and the lot naturally fell to the junior subaltern. Intensely hot in June, I lived and worked in a small stifling room with no fan, in which the furniture consisted of a camp bed and table with a hurricane oil lamp, which gave little light. On call for 24 hours, often when I got to sleep at night, a signaller would arrive with another message for coding or decoding. Reluctantly I would emerge from under a mosquito net and return to the glimmer of the oil lamp, and the mosquitoes. As many of the messages were about Nadir Khan, at least I was kept well informed of his movements, and particularly enjoyed his scurry from Thal.

That brief taste of staff work made an unfortunate impression, for I decided never to be a staff officer, preferring an active, outdoor life with a battalion. Years later I realised that even in the army the pen is mightier than the sword, and senior rank difficult to attain without staff experience. Anxious for the future I then decided to take the Staff College examination just before reaching the age limit, but I had missed the opportunity for adequate preparation. A last minute cram enabled me to qualify, but not high enough for me to obtain a vacancy in a highly competitive examination.

My happy release from ciphers came in mid-June, when the battalion was ordered to Hangu, half way to Thal. Relieved in order to accompany it, my first task was to load stores and baggage on the troop train. When the work was completed I felt extremely ill; I was examined by a medical officer and suspected of having cholera, as there was a serious epidemic of that disease, with several deaths occurring every day. Showing suspicious symptoms, I was put in an isolation tent.

Very ill, I was not helped by the exhausting heat, from which the tent offered little protection. However, after a few days I improved; which indicated that the complaint was not cholera but dysentery. That permitted my being moved to the improvised hospital building, which provided more protection from the scorching sun, and in shade temperatures which reached 120°F. To relieve congestion the hospital discharged me a few weeks later, still far from fit; and my return to Dehra Dun coincided with that of the battalion. The 3rd Afghan War was over at a cost of 236 British and Indian killed, 615 wounded and 566 deaths from cholera. Luckily the fire was put out before it became a conflagration.

Had I been given a few weeks' convalescence in the cool of the hills, I might have made a complete recovery. But on the plains in the humid heat of the monsoon the dysentery returned. As no hospital for officers existed in Dehra Dun, I remained in the bungalow, with my bearer, Indian servant, doing his best as nurse. I was also greatly helped by the kindness and cheerful company of Lieutenant John Williams, who shared the bungalow. My condition got steadily worse, and at the end of a fortnight, the battalion medical officer sent me up to the British Military Hospital in Mussoorie.

Medicine had not then found the answer to dysentery, starvation seemed to be the main part of the cure, and after a long period of very restricted diet I was quite emaciated. In the Second World War I contracted dysentery on a few occasions, but modern sulpha drugs cured me in a few days. The disease is endemic in India due to poor sanitation and many flies, and in such countries this modern cure is a great blessing.

In the Himalayas, overlooking Dehra Dun, Mussoorie was a popular summer resort at an altitude of 6,600 feet, with temperatures degrees cooler than down below. At last I was in a hospital with a trained staff, even to British Q.A. nurses, who looked very smart in their red capes. This was the service which my sister joined later.

With facilities for proper diet and treatment I soon began to recover, and on discharge my doctor had the good sense to recommend me for a month's sick leave in Mussoorie. Most anxious to get fit, I walked and rode as much as possible and, when stronger, played tennis. At the beginning of October I rejoined the 2/9th in Dehra Dun, somewhat ashamed at being off duty for so long.

Following the intense heat of summer the plains were becoming cooler. The monsoon rain had ended, and even at midday the temperature was bearable. Officers were beginning to return from long leave, and for me there were new faces in the mess. With lumps of *gur*, brown cane sugar, I hurried to Flint's stable. When bought he looked thin and underfed, but now he appeared too fat and under exercised, for the *syce* (groom) had obviously done no more than give him a gentle stroll each day. Later in the riding school I found he had forgotten the little that I had taught him, and was more obstreperous than ever.

The C.O., Lt.-Colonel H. F. Collingridge, was back from leave, and, as I had not met him, was summoned to his office, where in my best starched uniform I presented myself. Lying on the table was my report from the Quetta Cadet College, which he discussed with me. He appeared satisfied. He then gave me a short sermon on the proud traditions and customs of the 9th Gurkha Rifles, which, though inspiring, added to an uneasy feeling that I had made a bad start, by spending three months out of five on the sick list. I hoped for better luck.

The *munshi* returned and congratulated me on remembering a few sentences of Gurkhali. I had only been back a fortnight trying to pick up the threads, when the peace was again disturbed, and it seemed I was not destined to stay with the 2/9th. The north-west frontier had remained uneasy after the Afghan War, and the Mahsuds and Wazirs were carrying out murderous raids across the border. Operations to curb their activities were unavoidable. A field force was being assembled, and the regiment was ordered to send two subalterns as reinforcements to Bannu; the choice fell on John and myself.

It was now a year since I had arrived in India, long enough to form first impressions. The intense heat of summer had been a shock, which I had not enjoyed. The hot season on the plains did not suit the health of many Britons, including myself, for I never became acclimatised; I normally felt well in April and worn out by September. Annual summer leave of two months,

c

spent in the hills, provided some relief, but the best tonic was eight months' long leave in Britain, about every four years.

At that time India had a rapidly increasing population of over three hundred million, divided roughly into Hindus 68 per cent, Muslims 22 per cent, and the rest Sikhs, Buddhists, Christians and others. These communities lived separately, and showed no desire to intermarry or integrate. In the past there had been integration, but this had been at the point of the sword, and by the abduction of women, a form of barbarism which I was to witness during the Punjab massacres of 1947. The purest descendants of the Muslim invaders are to be seen in the north-west, now West Pakistan, among the Pathans and Western Punjabis, who have a Middle East appearance. In the rest of India Islam had spread by conversion and mixed marriages, so that the Muslims there are more closely related in race to the Hindus.

It was generally possible to distinguish the different communities by their dress, especially the headdress and hairstyle. The easiest to recognise was the Sikh, with his long hair and rolled beard. The Muslim favoured a trimmed beard and in certain regions bobbed hair, whereas the Hindu generally shaved and kept his hair short with a top-knot. Except for the Sikh, the distinctive hair styles tended to disappear in later years with the adoption of western haircuts. The northern Muslim generally wrapped his turban round an embroidered *kullah* (skull cap), or wore an Astrakhan cap, while the Hindu tied his turban without a *kullah* or favoured a Gandhi cap. It was noticeable that the Sikhs, like men of mediaeval times, sometimes carried swords. Ostensibly a religious symbol, this mode of dress also had practical value in matters like getting the best seat on a bus or train, as unarmed rivals tended to give way.

The only Buddhists I met were on the Tibetan border, and are described later. The small Christian community were divided into Indian converts, and Anglo-Indians of mixed blood. The latter were western in dress and habits, and generally found employment in the junior civil service, police and railway. Mixed marriages between Britons and Indians were rare, but they must have been more prevalent in earlier times, when slow travel made India more remote from Britain.

Purdah or the seclusion of women was very marked, especially among the Muslims of the north-west. Women were less restricted further east and south in the predominantly Hindu regions, which showed that there they were safer, with less need for the protection of *purdah*. The confinement and restriction imposed on women, especially in a stifling climate, were unhealthy and depressing. With *purdah* and little or no education, their talents were wasted and their seclusion did much to hinder progress in India.

There were many rich men in India, apart from the fabulously rich maharajas, rajas and nawabs who ruled much of the country and maintained lavish courts. A prosperous middle class also flourished, such as merchants in the towns and big landlords in the country. The wealthy lived comfortably in big houses with servants, and could be seen of an evening taking the air in their horse carriages. But at the bottom of the social scale, most of the people laboured in town and village for little reward, and lived in abject poverty. The main reason for poverty and hunger was the birth rate, with which national resources could not keep pace. Teenage marriage was general, and with no birth control families were very large.

The caste system also prevented people from improving their lot, by restricting the enterprise of the lower castes and the untouchables. I had a distressing experience of this caste system. The bearer I engaged in Dehra Dun, a low caste Hindu, was a splendid man who had served with officers of the 9th for many years, and the Gurkhas had never objected to him. But when I later joined a high caste Hindu regiment, since Dogra mess orderlies objected to working with him, I was forced to discharge him. Strangely, they had no objection to working with a Muslim. Despite their harsh attitude the orderlies were kindly men, so was the battalion Pandit or priest. They apologised to me, but said they had no choice.

In many areas food production depended on seasonal rain which was unreliable, and good harvests alternated with bad.

The Government carried out many projects to improve and increase agriculture, notably the extensive irrigation canal network in the Punjab, which utilised the water of the great rivers and was the largest canal system in the world. The desert to the south was turned into fertile farmland, and thousands of ex-soldiers and others settled there, but the demand for land always remained unsatisfied.

The tropical climate with its intense summer heat tended to slow up activity and productivity. The relatively small revenue of the country made it impossible to finance a welfare state to alleviate the suffering of the poor, except in genuine famine. Generally the only insurance for the poor was their own, most noble, joint family system, whereby relations helped each other.

For us life in most ways was comfortable, but in some respects primitive. The officers' mess was a substantial building, and, as the permanent home of the regiment, comfortable and attractive. As usual in India there were too many servants; the permanent mess staff, officers' personal bearers who waited at table, and soldier orderlies acting as wine waiters.

The bachelors shared a bungalow, in which each had a bedroom and bathroom, with cheap furniture hired from the bazaar. Cold water in an earthen jar was provided from a well by the *bhisti* (water carrier), and hot water was heated outside in a tin can on an open wood fire. The toilet consisted of a commode, which was manually cleared to an incinerator by the *mehtar*, who also did the sweeping.

As a subaltern I had two whole time servants, a bearer and a *syce*, and shared the *bhisti* and *mehtar* with others. Their wages were low, but each did very little work. One man could easily have done the work of all four, and increased his remuneration accordingly, but the caste system prevented this, and it would have meant fewer jobs, where much unemployment existed. Domestic service with the British was popular, with no shortage of applicants, and generally a happy relationship existed between master and servant, with loyalty on both sides.

A matter I had hardly considered before joining the army was finance, but now responsible for my own cheque book, I realised I was not in a lucrative profession. On Rs425 a month, about £28, it was barely possible to pay rent, servants, hire of furniture, mess and club bills, to buy clothes and uniform, and to keep Flint. I was determined to remain solvent, but clearly could not save for home leave. At that time we had to pay our own fares by sea, and without some money in the bank leave was impossible. It seemed that the only place where a subaltern could save for home leave was on the frontier, away from the heavier expenses of a peace station, and with field service concessions such as free rations for self, servant and horse. That is where I was going.

CHAPTER II

LIFE ON THE NORTH-WEST FRONTIER

On the British side of the Indo-Afghan frontier, from Chitral to Baluchistan, stretched a belt of independent tribal territory, varying in width from 10 to 100 miles. The boundary between that and administered territory was known as the administrative border. In the North-West Frontier Province the border roughly coincided with the edge of the Indian plain, and the start of the hills and mountains rising to Afghanistan. The people who lived both sides of the border were the Pathans, who spoke their own language Pushtu. Those who lived on the administered side were called the *cis*-border Pathans, and those on the tribal side the *trans*-border Pathans.

From time immemorial the hungry hillmen had raided the fertile farmlands of the plains, and to prevent that by administering up to the Afghan frontier would have meant disarming the *trans*-border tribes against bitter opposition. Having disarmed them, it would have been necessary to protect them against the armed

Afghan tribes by closely defending the Afghan frontier, which instead of solving the problem would have merely pushed it further west, at far greater cost and loss of life.

The rugged hills and mountains beyond the border were as ideal for defence as was Monte Cassino in the Second World War, with similar natural strongholds everywhere. In defending them a million elusive warriors would never have tired, and when hard-pressed would have taken refuge in Afghanistan, only to return again and again. For strategic reasons the half-dozen mountain passes between Afghanistan and India had to be held, but the occupation of all tribal territory would have meant a costly increase to the peace-time British-Indian Army. In the event of an international threat, as happened in two world wars, such an army of occupation would have been tied down far from the decisive battlefields. Against incessant raiding a cheaper safeguard had to be found.

The system adopted was to provide normal government and administration up to the border, beyond which the tribesmen were free to manage their own affairs, and helped with allowances on condition that they kept the peace. If the agreement was broken by persistent raiding, punitive action was taken. This appears more like a deal with criminals than a relationship between nations, yet offered a humane solution. Without help the *trans*-border Pathans could not subsist on their barren land, and for centuries had plundered the *cis*-border villages, but when British rule was extended to the border, protection of those villages had to be provided.

Independent to run their own affairs, and aided by allowances, it was hoped the tribesmen would leave their neighbours in peace. The arrangement was preferable to military occupation of tribal territory, and forced administration of a hostile people, but met with varying success, and least in Waziristan. With a criminal gang protection money does not always ensure peace, and violence breaks out either because the gang wants excitement or more money, as happened with the Pathans. Life was dull in the mountains, and new generations of restless young warriors were always anxious to show their mettle and emulate

their fathers. They were led astray by the old Pathan proverb :
'Nothing pays better than a good raid.'

In early days the punitive expeditions had to set off from
administered territory following the rough camel tracks, and
to reach the offending tribe often meant long marches through
the territory of others, with the undesirable result of extending
the conflict. It therefore became necessary to build strategic roads,
and place striking forces in areas which refused to desist from
raiding. The tribes were still left free to manage their own
affairs, and the primary aim of the striking force, like that of a
police force, was not to punish but to deter. Even when crimes
were committed, fines, in money and rifles, were preferred to the
last resort of destroying villages.

The forces across the border had a dual role; some defended
the passes into India such as the Khyber and the Kurram, and
others occupied strategic points to deter or act against raiders.
Those forces consisted of the regular army, and lightly armed
scouts or militia capable of dealing with small hostile groups.
The scouts were permanently resident, unlike army units which
were constantly changing. Apart from reducing the number
of regular troops, scouts, composed of Pathans from both sides
of the border, were more acceptable to the tribesmen, and so a
pacifying influence. Unfortunately the *trans*-border Pathans
in the scouts deserted on occasions with their arms to join the
hostiles, their kith and kin, which meant that Pathan scouts alone
could not be trusted to police tribal territory.

The tribes with whom I became acquainted inhabited Waziristan and the Kurram Valley. In the Kurram were the friendly
Turis and Bangash. Because of their reliability the Turis were
strongly represented in the Kurram Militia, and the Bangash
recruited both in the army and the militia.

Very different were the tribes in Waziristan to the south,
which during my service was the storm centre of the frontier,
due to the warlike character of the two main tribes, the Wazirs
and Mahsuds. Two smaller tribes the Dauds and Bhitannis
gave little trouble.

The smallest tribe, the peaceful Dauds, inhabited the lower

Tochi valley, were harassed by the surrounding Wazirs, and therefore well disposed towards the British because of their protection.

Bhitannis lived in the foothills between the rivers Tochi and Gumal, a very unhealthy malarious tract, which explains why they were not a robust tribe. Inclined to peace they were careful not to provoke or resist Mahsuds passing through their territory to raid the settled districts.

The country of the Wazirs, the largest tribe, stretched in a semicircle from the Tochi to the Gumal. They gave constant trouble by raiding into the plains, sniping, ambushing troops, and occasionally by more concerted attacks.

Arch brigands of the frontier and the scourge of Waziristan were the Mahsuds, who, surrounded by the others, lived in the central highlands, where, above the malarial belt, they enjoyed a temperate and invigorating climate. The troops in that area at Razmak, altitude 6,500 feet, were the healthiest in India, and equally fit for the fray were their neighbours the Mahsuds. Held in fear and distrust by all, with savage cruelty they raided the settled districts, and with equal zest plundered their neighbours.

As Brigade Intelligence Officer at Razmak in 1934, I was occasionally sent on a reconnaissance with an escort of Mahsud *khassadars*. They were tribesmen hired for various protection duties, with their own arms and loosely organised under their own leaders; a surrender to blackmail by hiring the men who would otherwise shoot at you. They were jovial, swashbuckling characters, with a cut-throat appearance and unreliable.

As Mahsuds were notoriously treacherous, with a record for murdering British officers, I regarded those escorts with some suspicion. I remember once asking a member of my escort what he did for a living, and without a moment's hesitation he said, "Steal". I remarked that the prospects seemed poor in such a barren country with everyone carrying a rifle. He replied, "The prospects are not bad if you cover a wide field. I steal from the Wazirs, the Bhitannis, the Powindahs (Afghan nomads), the villages in the plains and", with a rougish grin, "from the British". He was not an isolated criminal in an otherwise orderly society, but a typical Mahsud.

In appearance I could not distinguish between a Mahsud and a Wazir. Tall and lean with hawkish features, they grew beards and wrapped their bobbed hair in greasy turbans. A loose shirt hung down to their knees over baggy cotton trousers gathered at the ankle, and on their feet were rope or leather sandals, ideal for moving fast on steep slopes. Their dirty clothes were perfect camouflage against the grey-brown background of the rocky hills, on which they were as nimble as goats. They liked fancy leather bandoliers and belts, for holding cartridges and a dagger, and to be without a rifle was to be undressed.

In religion they were Muslims, but, being illiterate and led by mullahs or priests with little education, interpreted their creed in a wild and fanatical way. Perhaps the most popular expression of their faith was a crusade against the infidel; Briton, Hindu or Sikh, but they could also turn against the neighbouring tribe over the ridge, or even the next-door family, appearing to live in a world of hate and feuds. Provided they turned towards Mecca five times a day and prayed, and met the demands of their mullahs, they were free to thieve and murder as they pleased. In murdering an infidel there was positive merit, and according to fanatical mullahs this was a passport to paradise.

The greatest menace to the life of the Pathan was *badal*, the law of retaliation, or the blood feud, which could exist between tribes, sub-tribes (*khels*) or families. Between tribes two common causes of dispute were grazing rights and water, and when in Razmak, sometimes we heard or saw Mahsuds and Wazirs shooting it out, after both had driven their flocks towards the same grazing ground. In a trivial dispute between neighbours, a fatal rifle shot might follow an argument, and the death could only be expiated by counter-murder. There were no police or law courts in tribal territory, and rough justice was enforced only by *badal*, which could continue until a family was wiped out, unless a settlement was made by a *jirga* (council of elders), on agreement to pay compensation. The best way to lessen violence within the clan was by uniting against a common enemy; another tribe or the British.

A comparison is interesting between the life of a *cis*-border

Pathan and that of his cousin across the border; between the blessings and burdens of civilisation and those of savage freedom. Taxes were the biggest burden of the *cis*-border Pathan, but for those he received many benefits and services. Against the raider he was closely defended by the Frontier Constabulary, and further afield by the Army and Frontier Scouts. From criminals he was protected by the police and the law courts, though he too had to observe the law. Hospitals, medical surgeries, schools and colleges were provided, not on the scale of a modern welfare state, but to the extent India could afford. Steady improvement was made in facilities such as roads, railways and canals. Employment was available in government services, the security forces and private fields. The *cis*-border Pathan, as a member of a civilised state, had the rights and liabilities of a citizen.

Some of those benefits appealed to the *trans*-border Pathan, but the price was too high, and he would rather fight to the death than pay taxes. A Mahsud or Wazir did not want to pay for security, for it was more manly to provide it himself; why bother with the law courts, when you could shoot your enemy? After a raid it would be humiliating to have his house searched for loot, or to be taken to jail in handcuffs. Today his attitude towards education has changed, but then it was considered more important to breed fine outdoor men, who could move fast on a hill and shoot straight.

Generally tribesmen were work shy, though some would accept casual labour for road making and maintenance, but much more popular than work on the roads was employment as *khassadars* to protect them; the very men who otherwise would attack the traffic were paid, virtually bribed, to guard it. Thus with tribal allowances, *khassadar*'s pay and road contracts, the tribesmen were subsidised to keep the peace, and in the circumstances it was the cheapest solution and perhaps the kindest.

On leaving the plains and entering the hills there were striking differences, noticeably that every man carried a rifle and a dagger, as if he feared for his safety. The friendly looks of India were left behind, for here they were piercing and hostile. To discourage highwaymen the hills on either side of the road were piqueted by troops or scouts. Creaking bullock or buffalo carts were no longer seen, and their place was taken by pack camels. Cattle were rare, as only hardy animals, like camels and goats, could live on the coarse and scanty grazing. The only habitations were fortified villages, army camps, and stone forts.

A tribal village looked like a cluster of miniature mediaeval forts, for each house was designed not only to contribute to the protection of the whole village, but also for defence against its next-door neighbours. A few rooms, a small courtyard and a dominating rifle tower were enclosed by high walls, in which the rifle loopholes also served as windows.

Watch towers were built even in the fields, for men were an easy target when working, which they did with loaded rifles slung on their shoulders, or stacked within immediate grasp. To keep watch a sentry would be seated near by or in a watch tower, scanning the hills for any suspicious movement. Across the border a different world existed, a dangerous one, in which it was necessary not only to be armed but loaded.

In 1919 Waziristan was even more hostile than usual, for the Mahsuds and Wazirs had promised to co-operate with the Afghans in the holy war. Attacks in the Tochi and South Waziristan tied down British troops, as did raids into the districts of Bannu and Dera Ismail Khan. In trying to stir up the frontier, the Afghans certainly succeeded with the Mahsuds and Wazirs, for they proved more effective as warriors than the Afghans themselves.

The tactics of the tribesmen followed the usual pattern. By attacking and ambushing small army or scout posts and patrols, they added to their store of arms and ammunition. There was a great increase in raiding, and in six months from May to November the Mahsuds and Wazirs carried out nearly two hundred raids in the border districts, killed over two hundred peaceful villagers, and wounded many more. The situation called for drastic action.

In May to avoid unnecessary dispersion during the encounter with the Afghans, isolated scout posts in both North and South

Waziristan had been withdrawn. In the north those posts included Datta Khel in the Upper Tochi, and Spinwam linking the Tochi and Kurram. Disturbed by the withdrawals, the Wazirs in the Tochi Scouts deserted with their arms and joined the hostiles, but fortunately that force had a strong element of loyal *cis*-border Pathans and therefore remained effective.

The situation in the Tochi was helped by the metalled road from Bannu to Dardoni, which enabled regular troops to be located at strategic points, where within striking distance of Wazir villages they acted as a deterrent. Their presence also had a steadying influence on the scouts, as was shown when their Wazirs deserted. During my stay in the Tochi the regular troops were disposed with an infantry brigade at Bannu and a battalion forward at Saidgi, the first staging post to Dardoni; a forward brigade at Dardoni with a battalion back at Idak, the second staging post. Staging posts were necessary in the days of animal transport.

Though the Tochi up to Dardoni had been brought under control, elsewhere in Waziristan the situation had deteriorated. In South Waziristan the withdrawal of forward scout posts was regarded as a sign of weakness, and ended disastrously. The posts evacuated at Wana and in the Gumal valley were garrisoned by South Waziristan Scouts, of whom the majority were Wazirs and Afridis. There were no supporting regular troops in the area to exercise a restraining influence, and when orders were received to withdraw, the Wazirs and Afridis mutinied.

With their escape cut off eastwards towards the border, eight British officers and a few hundred loyal scouts under Major G. H. Russell set off for Fort Sandeman in the Zhob valley, hotly pursued by a swarm of Wazir and Mahsud tribesmen. During the long and exhausting withdrawal in intense heat, five British officers were killed and two wounded. Major Russell, who conducted the operation with the greatest skill and courage, was lucky to survive.

Because of their unreliability the South Waziristan Scouts were disbanded, but a few years later were reconstituted with a stronger element of loyal *cis*-border Pathans. After his experience at Wana Major Russell would have been understood for quitting Pathans, yet he undertook the task of reconstitution.

In August 1919, when peace was signed with the Afghans, the Wazirs and Mahsuds were bitterly disappointed with their allies and determined to fight on. Regarding the withdrawals from Datta Khel and Wana as major victories, they were well pleased with themselves. Through desertions and encounters they had greatly increased their armament of modern rifles and reserves of ammunition, and numerous raids across the border were proving fruitful and exciting.

Having disposed of the Afghans the army now had to contend with the tribes in Waziristan, and planned to deal first with the Upper Tochi Wazirs, then the Mahsuds in the centre, and finally the Wana Wazirs in the south. If the Mahsuds were beaten there would be little resistance from the Wana Wazirs.

To impress the Tochi Wazirs it was decided to show them that we could occupy the Upper Tochi at will. A mobile column was therefore assembled at Dardoni, a few weeks after I arrived in the Tochi, as the small striking force there was not strong enough for a deep penetration into tribal territory. Without opposition the column reached Datta Khel, where a *jirga* of Wazirs accepted peace terms.

The main Mahsud strongholds were Makin and Kaniguram in the high central uplands, to which no approach road existed, and the only feasible access was up the valley and narrow defiles of the river Takki Zam. On 11 December, a column consisting of two Indian infantry brigades, under Major General (later General) Sir Andrew Skeen, advanced from Jandola. After two months of bitter fighting, especially at the Ahnai Tangi, a narrow gorge between towering cliffs, Makin was reached by the middle of February. A few weeks later the column reached its final objective, Kaniguram; peace terms were accepted by the Mahsuds; and to ensure their observance a permanent garrison was established at Ladha near by.

Although peace had been made with the tribesmen, it was a vague term in Waziristan, and while for a time large scale attacks ceased, minor attacks and ambushes continued. In the next few years the policy which had proved successful in the Tochi was extended to the rest of Waziristan. Striking forces of regular troops were based at Razmak and Wana, and strategic roads constructed to link the Tochi, Central and South Waziristan.

The roads enabled quick concentration against tribes who refused to keep the peace, and also in later years served a nobler purpose. The tribesmen took very readily to owning and driving lorries, and the military roads gradually became commercial highways. When raiding failed to pay, the tribesmen turned to trade. From the higher mountains wood, and from other parts sheep, goats, wool, hides, all had a price in the markets of Bannu and Dera Ismail Khan, and therefore bandits out of work clubbed together to buy a lorry and engage in trade.

With the British providing free roads, lorries were cheaper and quicker than slow moving camels, and also safer, as the long straggling camel caravans were easy to attack. Each time I returned more tribal lorries were plying; in the wake of the mobile columns, the roads slowly brought civilisation to Waziristan. When I first arrived tribal lorries were yet to come, and camels still swayed along the tracks and river beds with their heavy burdens, as they had done for centuries.

*   *   *

That was the background when I began life as a subaltern on the frontier. When John Williams and I reported for duty at Bannu, the only Gurkhas in the Tochi were two platoons of 3rd Bn. 151st Punjabi Rifles at Idak, and so we were sent to join that battalion. In a Ford truck we both began the journey up the Tochi valley, while Flint and the *syce* had to follow by road convoy.

The road, strange and exciting, after leaving fertile Bannu traversed an arid stony tract as far as Saidgi. Marching towards the hills was a supply convoy of mule carts and pack camels, with its escort of troops, and heading for Bannu in the opposite direction a caravan of Wazir camels loaded with firewood, which would be traded for food and clothing. The accompanying tribes-men looked wild and unwashed, but walked with a swagger-ing gait. To encourage that kind of trade was the best antidote to raiding, and meant providing safe roads and staging camps.

Saidgi at the end of a day's march, the first staging camp, was perched on a cliff overlooking the River Tochi, at the entry to the Shinki defile. It was the most unpopular camp in the Tochi, intensely hot in summer with not a tree or vestige of shade, with anopheles mosquitoes breeding in the river bed, and a bad record for malaria. Beyond the camp was a steep ridge of rock, which rose like a forbidding rampart guarding tribal territory; those who passed through the Shinki, or gateway, did so at their peril.

On entering the Shinki defile we left behind the peaceful villages, and wide cultivated stretches of Bannu District, and crossed into Waziristan. Visible on the hills overlooking the road were the *sangars* (stone breastworks) of the road piquets, which confirmed that the road was not safe. The tribesmen had no artillery, *sangars* were adequate against rifle fire, and easily con-structed from stones lying everywhere.

Near the exit of the defile was the 'Beau Geste' fort of Khajuri, with mud and stone walls, and towers at the corners. Soon I was to become the commander of that little fort, which acted as parent to the road piquets, of which those near by were occupied during the daytime and those at a distance held permanently.

In the Tochi valley beyond were the villages of the peaceful Dauds, bordered on both sides towards the hills by the hamlets of the less peaceful Wazirs. Where water could be diverted along channels from the river and streams there was cultivation. With modern engineering the irrigation could have been greatly in-creased, and the cultivated area extended as in the settled dis-tricts, but that was possible only with efficient administration, unacceptable to the tribesmen. Beyond the belt of cultivation small herds of camels and goats were grazing on the sparse scrub and coarse grass. The woolly baby camels looked very attractive on long, spindly legs, gambolling near their parents, who appeared worn out with hard work and scanty fodder.

For several miles the road skirted the north side of the valley, then climbed a low ridge before dropping into Idak, second staging camp, our destination and home for several months. The 3/151st occupied the old fort and some meagre mud huts. More huts accommodated a squadron of the 31st Lancers, and empty tents for units in transit completed a typical frontier camp.

The truck deposited us in the fort, which housed the officers and one company. The mess had none of the luxury of that at Dehra Dun, comprising two small mud plastered rooms, with camp furniture designed to fold up, and load on to a mule cart, or a couple of camels, in minutes.

We went over to the office to report, first to Captain John Wainwright, the Adjutant, and then to Lt.-Colonel George Renny the C.O., whom we were soon to know well. John was always kind and helpful, even to the last joined subaltern, while George, large and jovial, was popular with his officers, and from them could count on a ready response. He had two loves in life, first his family in England, and second the Dogras; he had come from the 38th Dogras. After briefly checking up on my experience, or lack of it, the Colonel asked if I played hockey, and I informed him that I was in the first eleven at the Cadet College. That pleased him and he called in Lieutenant Roley Ingram-Johnson, the sports officer, and said, "Bristow plays hockey, try him out this afternoon". Roley became a friend for life, and the only member of the 3/151st with whom I was able to maintain contact throughout my service, and until he died 49 years later.

I was allotted a small room without windows and like a dungeon; the old fort was built not for comfort, but to keep out bandits. My only possessions were one trunk of clothes, a bedding roll and some camp furniture, but when scattered around, the dungeon looked quite homely. At the age of nineteen that was high adventure, and I wanted nothing more.

3/151st Punjabi Rifles struck me as different from 2/9th Gurkha Rifles, who had long experience with many battle honours, mature traditions, and a homogeneous composition of

Gurkhas. The 3/151st was still new, with less than two years' experience and one battle honour, Palestine 1918. Composed of drafts from other regiments and six different classes, the battalion was still in process of becoming a united team. During expansion of the Indian Army in the First World War, the 3/151st was one of the last battalions to be raised, which was done in Palestine, where it took a minor part in the last campaign.

For a battalion to have six classes was unusual in the Indian Army and a wartime accident. It was composed as follows: 'A' Company, half Punjabi Mussalmans, half Gurkhas, from the Guides Infantry; 'B' Company, mostly Dogras, a platoon of Garhwalis, from the 38th Dogras; 'C' Company, Punjabi Mussalmans from the 59th Scinde Rifles; 'D' Company, half Rajputs, half Ahirs, from the 98th Infantry. Such a rare mixture in one unit presented a unique opportunity to become acquainted with several classes of the Indian Army, all different in character and customs. Because of my connection with Gurkhas I was posted to 'A' Company, commanded by Captain Henry Fagnani.

Recently arrived from Palestine, and almost entirely composed of young officers and soldiers, the battalion was unacquainted with the frontier and mountain warfare. The only prewar regular officers were the Colonel and Major Thomas Digby, and it rested with them to pass on their experience.

Though sad at leaving the 2/9th, I relished the change from parade ground life in Dehra Dun to that of the frontier, and even more the beginning of a cold winter, which fully restored my health. We had a perfect training ground for making troops hard and fit; and soon I could climb hills with the best.

In 'A' Company the Punjabi Mussalmans (P.M.s) and Gurkhas were an odd combination, as they were quite different in appearance and character. Though on good terms they did not mix off duty, and I formed the impression that Gurkhas were happier in their own one-class regiments. The P.M.s were lean and tall with sharp features, independent in character, not so naturally disciplined as the Gurkhas, but brave and reliable soldiers. They welcomed me by an invitation to a meal, which

D

showed that, unlike Hindus they were not defiled by eating with a Christian.

Our task in Idak was to defend the staging camp, and the road half way to Saidgi and half way to Dardoni. A large part of the battalion was employed manning Khajuri Fort and the permanent road piquets, and when mule cart and pack camel supply convoys were using the road, the rest of the battalion moved out to reinforce the road piquets. As every cart or camel load was a prize worth having to the Pathans, convoys offered a great temptation to an attack. With the constant danger of ambush every move by the troops had to be tactically sound, which provided splendid training for young novices like myself.

Elaborate arrangements were made to protect the camp. On the overlooking hills were the camp piquets to prevent sniping, especially at night. Circling the camp was a breast-high stone wall, protected by two double aprons of barbed wire, and with a bastion every hundred yards for the perimeter piquets. By day only some were manned, each mounting a single sentry, but to guard against a sudden rush at night all the perimeter piquets were occupied, each mounting two sentries. The huts or tents of the infantry were near the perimeter, so that it could be manned in seconds, and every man slept with his rifle beside him. At sundown the quarter guard bugler sounded retreat, and all stood-to, to ensure that every man knew his alarm post for the night.

Riding and hockey were the only two recreations available at Idak, which suited me perfectly. Transport then was on an animal basis, with hundreds of mules and horses to be exercised, which was done on a litter track round the perimeter. It was too dangerous to ride beyond the camp piquets, and gallops had to be confined to the litter track, but fortunately the cavalry had some schooling paddocks, in which I spent many pleasant hours trying to improve Flint's wild habits. On road protection I often had to gallop long distances, and he became a vital partner in my job. As a member of the battalion team I played hockey regularly, the favourite Indian Army game, and occasionally we played in tournaments against other teams in Bannu, Saidgi and Dardoni, which made a pleasant change.

Only once was the whole battalion in action, and it happened soon after I joined. South of Idak, and across the River Tochi, a mountain called Zer rises another 1,700 feet above the valley. Tom Digby had taken 'C' Company out for an exercise on the lower slopes of Zer, but got further away from camp than was prudent. The ever watchful Tori Khel Wazirs saw their opportunity, and about fifty of them cut off his line of withdrawal. He could have fought his way out, but not without heavy casualties, and wisely helioed to the fort for help. (A helio is a visual signalling device to reflect the light of the sun, using morse code.)

On hearing the quarter guard bugler sound the alarm, we donned our equipment and turbans and ran to the parade ground, thinking it was a practice; in action British officers wore turbans like the men to avoid being conspicuous targets. Only when addressed by the C.O. did we realise that the alarm was real. After briefly explaining the situation, he detailed an advanced guard, and the battalion moved towards Zer. On wading the Tochi and approaching the mountain, we could hear rifle fire.

The advanced guard secured a knoll at the foot of the slope, and the battalion moved into its shelter, while the officers followed the C.O. to the top of the knoll to view the ground and receive orders. These were for 'A' and 'B' Companies to attack up a very steep slope, and secure a ridge to outflank the Wazirs, and for 'D' Company to remain in reserve. With many employed on road and camp piquets, companies were only at half strength. In the attack I led with the P.M.s on the right, and John Williams with the Dogras on the left, while Henry Fagnani followed in support with the Gurkhas.

The Wazirs soon re-acted to our attack, and moving away from 'C' company appeared in increasing numbers on the ridge which was our objective. Their fire was not very accurate and mostly went overhead, but occasionally one of our men was hit. As we were without artillery or even mortar support it was a fight between riflemen, in which the Wazirs had the great advantage of height. As we closed the gap there was much abusive yelling by the Wazirs, to which the P.M.s and Dogras replied with their own stirring war cries; a kind of war of nerves.

John and I reached the line where, according to the book, you fix bayonets and charge; and therefore behind convenient boulders, we formed up to assault. I noticed that the old Dogra Subedar Major, Jai Singh I.D.S.M., leaving the safety of his proper place with battalion headquarters, had joined us. With revolver drawn and encouraging his Dogras, he intended to charge with them, and so set an inspiring example. To our surprise firing by the Wazirs slackened, and they could be seen pulling out carrying some casualties; the gleam of bayonets had decided the war of nerves in our favour. Just as we were about to charge the ridge Henry arrived out of breath, having run up the hill, and ordered a withdrawal, an anticlimax.

Apparently we had drawn the Wazirs off 'C' Company, who were now clear, and had achieved our aim. As peace terms had only just been accepted by the Tochi Wazirs, George Renny did not wish to be held responsible for trailing his coat on Zer and restarting the war, which might have happened had he lingered there, and allowed the Tori Khel to gather for a major clash. With heavy fighting continuing in South Waziristan, peace in the Tochi was most desirable, and so having rescued 'C' Company, George decided to withdraw. To our surprise, the tribesmen did not follow up according to tradition; they had had enough.

On the way back I was passing through a patch of tall reeds in the river bed, when I heard a shout and a shot a few yards ahead. On running forward I saw a jubilant little Garhwali standing over a prostrate, wild looking Wazir, who was breathing his last. To get a rifle, and armed only with a large dagger, that foolhardy man had concealed himself in the path of withdrawal of a whole battalion; luckily for him the Garhwali had seen him in time.

George was delighted with his minor battle, and the experience gave a new battalion more confidence. No mistakes had been made, and 'C' Company had been extricated from a dangerous trap, which might have cost many more casualties than the few incurred. It was the first time many of us had been under fire, the best training of all. Subedar Khan Bahadur and the P.M.s of 'A' Company held a victory dinner, at which I was a guest of honour, and felt very elated.

The Political Tehsildar at Idak, our source of intelligence, reported that the Tori Khel lost several men on Zer, and true to the Pathan law of *badal*, intended to take revenge. We did not have long to wait. On road open days a platoon went out from Idak along the Bannu road, established a piquet at milestone 25 where the high ground ends, and another at milestone 24 in the valley beyond. They were both kept under observation from the permanent piquet on Hill 3176 north of the road. Soon after the encounter on Zer, the permanent piquet helioed that the further road piquet had been ambushed.

In camp a British officer and one platoon of 35 men were kept at short notice to move in emergency, and on that day I happened to be on duty with a platoon of Dogras. We ran the two miles to the nearer road piquet, and panting by my side was old Subedar Fateh Singh. Looking down the road we could see and hear the survivors holding off the Wazirs, and so, making use of cover, we spread out and stalked forward to engage them.

As we drew close a fire fight developed, and soon the tribesmen began to fall back northwards towards the Mir Ali hills, carrying some casualties. At that stage the Squadron of 31st Lancers arrived, dismounted and took up a position away to our left, from where they could harass the retreating Wazirs by fire. I was disappointed not to see a cavalry charge, but the ground was too broken. That was the only time that I saw horse cavalry in action, and felt that horses were much too vulnerable in battle even against Pathan rifle fire, yet Indian cavalry kept their horses for another twenty years.

It only remained for me to clear up the battlefield. The leading half of the piquet, six Rajputs and Ahirs, had all been killed at short range by the first volley of the ambush, and their rifles stolen. Following the leaders, the piquet commander Naik (Corporal) Harphul Singh had managed to dive for cover, and though isolated had valiantly kept the Wazirs at bay for some time, until killed with a dead Wazir almost touching him. In trying to get Harphul's rifle this man had lost his life and his own rifle, which was added to our mess trophies. The supporting half of the piquet, six Dogras under L/Naik Indar Singh dropped behind cover, and held off about forty Wazirs until we arrived. Two Dogras were wounded, but all were full of fight.

Because we were forbidden to start any shooting, the tribesmen had the great advantage of surprise, as shown on Zer and in the ambush, but on both occasions the battalion had re-acted well, and given a good account of itself. Harphul Singh was awarded a posthumous Indian Order of Merit, and Indar Singh an Indian Distinguished Service Medal. Presumably the Wazirs had decided that the 3/151st was not easy prey, for during the remainder of our stay in the Tochi they kept their distance, and we suffered only from occasional sniping.

While at Idak I enjoyed my first independent command at Khajuri Fort, which at a youthful age made me feel very important. With a company I was responsible for the protection of a section of the road, which included manning and supplying the road piquets. As life in the fort was very restricted, I spent much of my time out visiting piquets, climbing hills and exploring the area.

Not far away was a recently deserted Wazir hamlet, from which the owners had moved to another grazing area, and I took out a patrol to study their living conditions. The half dozen houses each had a rifle tower and a few small rooms, which were dark, damp and airless, almost like caves. The air inside was filled with an unpleasant odour of unwashed clothes and humanity, and we were attacked by swarms of fleas. The small stony fields surrounding the hamlet could have grown little food, which must have come mainly from flocks grazing with difficulty on the almost bare hills. No wonder the men's thoughts turned to plunder, goaded as they were by their hungry women and children.

After the winter in Idak the battalion moved on to Dardoni, a welcome change in scene and climate, and at 3,000 feet we could look forward to a somewhat cooler summer. The march took us deeper into the hills, which rose higher, though they remained almost bare of vegetation below 4,000 feet. Above this altitude the higher slopes caught the scanty rain, resulting in more plant life, particularly small bushy trees of holly oak.

For several miles the road was hemmed in by steep hills, and then entered a wide flat valley at Miranshah, the headquarters of the Tochi Scouts, who occupied a large, impressive fort, with an attractive garden near by, an oasis in an arid landscape. About a mile beyond was the hutted army camp of Dardoni.

Whereas Idak was merely a one battalion station and a staging camp, Dardoni contained most of the brigade and the striking force. Located there were brigade headquarters, two battalions, a mountain battery carried on pack mules, and a field company of engineers. One battalion was needed to protect the camp and man the permanent road piquets, leaving, for the striking force, one battalion, the mountain battery and a strong contingent of scouts.

The bigger garrison provided healthy rivalry in work and sport, and wider social life. The other battalion was 2nd Bn. 69th Punjabis, with whom we were soon on very friendly terms. Entertainments like a cinema were non-existent, radio and television belonged to the future, and so the evenings could be dull. As women were not allowed beyond Bannu for safety reasons the community was entirely male, and social life depended mainly on sport and entertaining friends at dinner.

The camp, recently built, was spacious and well planned. In the centre was an officers' square with messes and quarters, surrounded by unit huts extending up to the perimeter wall, outside which were the parade and sports grounds. The perimeter was guarded in the usual way, but as the camp was not overlooked, an outer ring of camp piquets was not necessary, which made duties lighter and the men enjoyed more nights in bed. Permanent road piquets had to be manned half way to Idak.

Facilities for games were good, including hockey grounds, tennis courts, and between Dardoni and the scout fort a rough polo ground. At hockey our rivals were the Gunners, the Sappers, and the 2/69th captained by Lieutenant Henry Tett, who became a close friend. As a result of much practice at Dardoni we won the Waziristan District Hockey Tournament, in which about twenty teams competed.

Even at games we were not allowed to forget the unfriendly Wazirs, for piquets had to be put out to protect the players. Once when playing the Gunners at hockey we were sniped, and Major Geoffrey Hill their C.O., who was playing, ordered out his little mountain guns, which the Gunners dashed off to bring into action. Within minutes shells were bursting on the hills, and their accuracy acclaimed by the spectators. When the snipers were dispersed the game continued.

The opportunity to play polo at last was a pleasant surprise, thanks to the generosity and enthusiasm of the Tochi Scout officers. With their mounted infantry company they possessed many sturdy ponies, of which those suitable were trained to play, and gladly lent to mount enough players. Polo should be played on grass, but there we had to make the best of dust and small stones, and when the ball was struck stones shot out like bullets, which added to the excitement of the game. As despite much schooling I failed to teach Flint to turn fast enough, I had to rely on borrowed ponies. After Dardoni I regret polo faded out of my life, being beyond my pocket.

When we reached Dardoni the operations against the Mahsuds to the south had ended and, except for minor incidents, Waziristan for a time became more settled. The striking force carried out regular exercises, but during our stay was never in action.

Two large permanent piquets had to be manned, Black Hill on the road to Idak, and Kalunja on the road to Datta Khel. Each was occupied by a company commanded by a British officer, and I spent a month first on Black Hill and later on Kalunja. In June 1919, the 41st Dogras had fought an action on the slopes of Black Hill, in which 2nd Lieutenant Percy Furley was killed. A popular cadet in my company at Quetta Cadet College, he tragically lost his life within six weeks of being commissioned; Black Hill had a bad reputation, in keeping with its name.

Each day the permanent piquet followed the same routine,

which would have been boring but for an element of danger, and the knowledge that any slackness might result in death. All of us stood-to alarm posts half an hour before dawn, as that was a likely time for attack. At first light the gate was opened and patrols searched the immediate vicinity for any lurking assassins. The day piquets then moved out to their positions along the road, after careful preparations for covering fire in case of ambush on the way. When the road was closed for traffic in the evening the road piquets returned, and the day ended with another stand-to at dusk.

Like most junior officers I enjoyed being on detachment and my own master. The responsibility for a hundred lives in hostile territory was excellent training, and sharing a small space with the men helped in getting to know them and in learning to speak their language. In winter with snow on the ground and icy winds, the open piquets were bitterly cold, and as our small tents had no heating arrangements there was little variation between outside and inside temperatures. Yet with much hill climbing we all kept remarkably fit.

Apart from being sniped at occasionally at night we had no trouble on Black Hill, but our successors the Tochi Scouts, despite being Pathans, were not so fortunate, as very soon after we handed over a day piquet was ambushed, and they lost a dozen men and rifles. In tribal territory a British rifle sold for £70, a fortune to a tribesman, and for that a Pathan was prepared to kill even a Pathan.

Kalunja Piquet was perched on a dominating peak and we enjoyed exceptionally fine views of the Upper Tochi and high mountains surrounding us. Soon after arrival a young Wazir brought me an invitation to tea from his father, a retired subedar of the Baluch Regiment, who lived in the hamlet down below. I found him a handsome, interesting old man, who enjoyed talking about his military service and British officers he knew, just as any other old soldier. Like most Pathans he had a great sense of humour. When the British evacuated the Upper Tochi in the Afghan War, he said that the Wazirs had burned all the scout posts between Miranshah and Datta Khel, except the one on the hill above his house. He threatened to shoot anyone who laid hands on it, to prove his loyalty, and to ensure the payment of his army pension. We both enjoyed a good laugh.

It was unfortunate that the Wazirs had proved treacherous on occasions, and were no longer recruited; for the fact that they were not trusted, and had lost their place in the fighting forces, added to their estrangement.

Some officers had left on postwar demobilisation, and I moved up to command 'B', the Dogra company. I began with doubts as to whether I should like serving with high caste Hindus and their religious taboos, but my fears were soon dispelled, for their prohibitions appeared to cause no serious problems. To give two examples: when eating they disliked others to approach them, but there was no need to do so; they regarded cattle as sacred, and it would have been a great insult to offer them beef, but it was quite easy to feed them on goat-meat. There was a simple answer to all their customs, about which they showed the greatest tact, and moreover as men of high caste set high standards in honesty, loyalty, good manners and life generally. British officers called Dogras the gentlemen of the Indian Army, which was a high compliment in an army so well behaved. I soon became deeply attached to fatherly old Subedar Fateh Singh and his Dogras.

With a good record we had hoped that the battalion would be retained in the peace-time army, and were greatly disappointed when, in February 1921, it was ordered to disband. The four companies returned to their parent battalions, but the officers were asked where they wished to go, and without hesitation I applied to remain with 'B' Company and to join the 38th Dogras; so did Roley Ingram-Johnson. George Renny who was returning to the 38th supported our applications, and we were delighted when posted to that battalion, which soon after was renamed 2nd Bn. 17th Dogra Regiment.

The disbandment of the 3/151st at Poona was for me a sad occasion, as with them I had become part of the Indian Army, and had graduated from novice to trained soldier.

*   *   *

Like most Indian Army officers I spent about a quarter of my service on the frontier, returning four times to Waziristan, and once to the Kurram. Except in 1937 my spells coincided with peaceful periods, and I took no part in major operations. The minor incidents continued, but accounts of them would add little to the picture already painted from my experience as a subaltern, and to avoid repetition these later visits will be covered very briefly.

In 1924, I accompanied the 2/17th Dogras to Tank and Manzai, where we spent two uneventful years protecting the supply road to Jandola and Wana. Lt.-Colonel Alec Kerr was commanding, and appointed me as his adjutant, a post coveted by junior officers, for it meant a hand in all battalion activities and never a dull moment.

The battalion spent the first eight months at Tank, regarded as the unhealthiest camp on the frontier, it lived up to its reputation, for within a few months Captain Alan Reiche, an outstanding officer, and several men died of pneumonia. The prevalence of that disease in winter was attributed to a thick layer of powdery dust, which, if disturbed by traffic or by the slightest wind, rose in a dense, suffocating cloud. During summer few escaped from malaria. Surrounded by peaceful tribes we were never called out in emergency, and our main problem was to keep the men fit. There were no regrets when the battalion moved to Manzai, situated on a low ridge overlooking the Tank plain. Away from the infectious dust, in a cleaner atmosphere, the battalion soon improved in health.

Climate plays a major part in the health and character of people. This was especially noticeable in India, where in many places, in a few hours, it was possible to drive from the sweltering plains and malaria, to the cool, bracing air of the mountains, away from the anopheles mosquito. A good example of this was Razmak our next frontier station during 1933–34, where the Mahsuds, living in the surrounding uplands, were full of vigour. Enjoying the climate of a hill resort the troops of Razmak Mobile Column were also wonderfully fit, which they needed to be with such aggressive neighbours.

Periodically, Razcol took to the hills and strategic roads, both to carry out training exercises and to support the political officers in striving for peace, by showing that we could retaliate against those who raided the border. Part of the time I acted as Brigade Intelligence Officer, and for the rest commanded a company, and this had meant little progress since 1921. Feeling that I had got into a rut, I decided on long leave to England to take the Staff College Entrance Examination, but just failed to pass high enough.

However, I met Elsa and returned with a wife, but we could not live together until the battalion left Razmak. Most bachelors enjoyed being on the frontier, and I certainly did, but marriage made a difference, for it meant long separations and maintaining two homes, or even three for those with children at school in Britain.

Columns operating from Razmak, Wana and Mir Ali helped to keep Waziristan at peace until 1936. Unfortunately the strategic roads did not penetrate the somewhat inaccessible Shaktu and Khaisora valleys, which were well placed for forays into the plains. Beyond the shadow of the mobile columns those valleys provided a natural stronghold for the next firebrand of Waziristan, the Fakir (holy man) of Ipi, a Tori Khel Wazir from Arsal Kot in the Shaktu Valley, who decided it was time for another holy war, and met with a ready response from a new generation of warriors. Numerous raids and incidents occurred, of which the worst was an ambush, in April 1937, of a motor convoy to Wana, in the narrow Shahur Tangi, in which we suffered 52 killed including 7 British officers, and 47 wounded.

To quell the rising, and construct a road into the hostile area, four brigades had to be brought up to reinforce the local columns. In the summer of 1937 Elsa and I were enjoying long leave in England, with two months remaining, when I received a cable ordering me to return, as the 2/17th had moved to the frontier. We caught the first ship back to India, and I rushed up to Waziristan, to find the battalion having a very dull time doing road protection at Tal-in-Tochi. We missed the main fighting, and on returning to Kamptee a few months later, I felt the loss of leave had been a vain sacrifice. With the Second World War ahead, it was my last leave in England before retiring in 1948.

In September 1941, I again returned to the frontier, to Thal-in-Kurram, the scene of Dyer's battle against the Afghans in 1919. I was then commanding a new battalion, the 6/17th Dogra Regiment, which had been given the task of helping to construct modern defences across the Kurram Valley.

By the autumn of 1941, the German *blitzkrieg* against Russia had advanced 500 miles to Rostov, within striking distance of the Caucasus. Had Russia collapsed like France, it was thought the German panzers might drive through Persia and Afghanistan towards India. In June 1940, Sir Winston Churchill had made his famous declaration that we would never surrender, and if necessary continue the struggle from our Empire overseas. The trenches and concrete emplacements in the Kurram were in keeping with that resolve.

At Thal the winter in tents, with snow on the ground, was bitterly cold, but digging trenches kept us all fit. Though the Germans did not get beyond Stalingrad, it was considered that the defences in the Kurram, and other north-west frontier passes, had not been wasted, for they showed our determination to defend India, and so proved to be a stabilising influence on the tribes throughout the war. The enemy who did reach the gates of India were the Japanese in Arakan and Assam, and as they were not met by concrete pillboxes, it seems those had been put in the wrong place; such is the uncertainty of war.

The digging was completed by January, when we were sent to Rawalpindi, and later ordered to mobilise for war and a move to Assam. That was cancelled as explained in Chapter V, and we returned very disappointed to Thal to become part of the permanent garrison. The Turi and Bangash tribesmen were at peace, not a shot was fired in anger, and we devoted ourselves to training on the surrounding hills, dominated by Khadimakh, where Dyer fought his last action against the Afghans.

Thal Fort in the summer of 1942 was airless and like an oven, and by September most of us were feeling somewhat jaded, when orders arrived for a move to Mir Ali in Waziristan, where a comfortable and modern camp had replaced Idak near by. For me in 23 years the wheel had gone full circle, for as a C.O. I was back in view of Zer mountain, where I had fought my first battle as a 2nd lieutenant. In normal times this would have been the fulfilment of ambition, but now I suffered a sense of guilt.

The war had been in progress for three years, my efforts to get the 6/17th and myself there had failed, it seemed that the battalion was committed to the frontier indefinitely, and so I clutched at a straw. The C.O. of the Dogra Machine Gun Battalion in the Middle East had been invalided to India, and I applied direct to the Military Secretary to replace him, pointing out that I was a qualified machine gunner. This method of applying for an appointment was forbidden, but I decided to risk the consequences. I received no reply, nor to my surprise a reproof.

The winter in Mir Ali was bracing, and we carried out much strenuous training both by day and night. When climbing the neighbouring hills, we must have provided tempting bait to our old friends, the Tori Khel, but they never attacked and appeared to be observing a gentlemanly truce. Perhaps they preferred us to the Germans or Japanese, and were prepared to hold their fire while we had our backs to the wall.

For three months I was made temporary commander of Bannu Brigade and Tochi Mobile Column, a new experience which I greatly enjoyed. About six months after I wrote to the Military Secretary, a letter arrived appointing me to command the M.G. Battalion; the inspiration had worked after all. The five happy years I spent with the 6/17th are described in more detail in Chapter V.

In April 1943, I left Waziristan for the last time. Since 1919 there had been steady improvement in the lot of the soldiers. Movement across the hills presented the same challenge, but road protection was much easier, as fast moving motor convoys, escorted by armoured cars, had replaced slow marching mule carts and camels, protected by soldiers on foot; a dangerous and exhausting task. There was greater comfort in camp and piquet. The officers' quarters and men's barracks in Mir Ali were well built with electric light and fans, a great advance on the tents, temporary huts and hurricane oil lamps of 1920. The open *sangars* of the permanent road piquets had been replaced by weatherproof stone towers.

Penetrating the mountain barriers, roads had brought the tribesmen into contact with civilisation, and they were becoming less wild. The roads, which at first they had bitterly resented, were later used regularly by themselves, with tribal lorries plying between Kaniguram, Makin, Datta Khel and Bannu carrying the produce of the hills and valleys in exchange for wheat, cloth and manufactured goods. It began to dawn on the tribesmen that work and trade were more rewarding and less hazardous than thieving.

Britons today visiting the frontier are well received, because their forebears had refrained from firing the first shot, fought by the rules, treated the enemy wounded, honoured agreements and above all built the roads.

CHAPTER III

LIFE IN A PEACE STATION

While periodically we served on the north-west frontier, the greater part of our lives was spent under more normal conditions in military cantonments, known in army language as peace stations.

Cantonments had been sited long before the days of quick motor transport, when troops had to march to the scenes of trouble. As the main trouble spots were the large towns and cities, cantonments had been located within a few miles of them. Usually they took the name of the town to which they were linked, thus the one near Jullundur City was called Jullundur Cantonment.

A cantonment also provided security for the local civil administration, which together with the police occupied an area known
as civil lines. Generally that was situated between cantonment
and town and also took the same name—Civil Lines Jullundur.

Towns were mainly ancient in layout and architecture, with
houses packed closely together and separated only by narrow
streets and lanes. As families became wealthier or increased in
number the tendency was to add another floor, so that many
of the buildings were several storeys high; the more important
or affluent the owner the higher the building. A house with a high
flat roof, not overlooked, was a luxury greatly desired, for in the
intense suffocating heat of summer people would sleep at night
on the roof. In default of modern plumbing and sewerage systems
night-soil had to be carted to incinerators, and therefore efficient
sanitation was sadly lacking; unpleasant smells pervaded the air
and flies swarmed.

In contrast to the towns, civil lines and cantonments were
well laid out with wide roads and generous spacing between
buildings, which were mostly of the one storey or bungalow type.
Although the system of sanitation was similar to that in the
towns, it was more strictly supervised and helped by less congestion.

Civil lines contained public offices, law courts, the treasury,
police barracks and the homes of officials. The area was extensive
at the headquarters of a Province, such as Lahore, fairly large at
the headquarters of a Civil Division such as Jullundur, and
smallest at the headquarters of a Civil District such as Ferozepore.

A cantonment was divided roughly into separate areas for
officers' residences, barracks for different units, a military dairy
farm, and a shopping centre called the Sadar Bazaar, which
provided a market not only for the garrison but also for the
surrounding villages. Unlike the rest of an orderly cantonment,
its bazaar was generally seething with people, *tongas* (one horse
cabs), cars and bullock carts. The noise and bustle were typical
of the East. On the periphery of a cantonment were parade
grounds, firing ranges, playing fields, and perhaps polo grounds
and a golf course. With a large garrison a cantonment comprised

1. Officers of the Dogra Regiment, reunion, 1932

2. British officers, 2nd Bn. Dogra Regiment, 1938—author middle row, seated on left

3. Junior Commander Elsa Bristow, Women's Auxiliary Corps (India)

4. Petworth : Our first home, Kamptee, 1934

5. Evening conference, Razmak Mobile Column, 1934

6. Tribal village near Razmak

7. Wazir tribesmen

8. Christmas shooting party near Kamptee, 1936. (Dogra Orderly Tulsi standing third from the right)

a self-contained town, and with a small garrison a self-contained village.

During 29 years, I resided in 15 different peace stations, attended army schools at several other places, and spent summer leave in various hill resorts. Long journeys by train were frequent, and sometimes these were by troop train carrying the whole battalion; like nomads we were constantly packing up to move on. Although Indian Army life was somewhat restricted, constant changes of scene helped to provide variety and to counter boredom.

So much movement might not appear economical, but it was necessary to keep troops fit, garrison the frontier, and provide reserves trained in mountain warfare. Except in the north-west, the Gurkha hill stations and a few other places, the hot climate of India was not conducive to vigour and military efficiency. A battalion kept indefinitely in central or southern India would deteriorate, and lack essential experience in frontier or mountain warfare. The policy, therefore, was to keep units circulating between healthy stations, unhealthy stations and the frontier, with a few years in each, so giving all an equal opportunity to remain fit and efficient.

For a bachelor living in the mess those moves caused little inconvenience, for even as a senior bachelor all my belongings could be packed in a few hours in half a dozen boxes. But it was very different for a married couple, for whom constant moves were generally a strain and a nuisance. On marriage our packages totalled about fifty and took days to pack, often working stripped to the waist in a temperature of 110°F.

As a warning to young officers the problems and difficulties of marriage were pointed out. Thirty was considered a suitable age for marriage, as then an officer was entitled to marriage allowance, and had usually attained the rank and pay of captain. Those, without private means, who married before thirty had difficulty in remaining solvent in a fighting unit, and often had to transfer to administrative services, with better pay and fewer expenses. The welfare of an Indian unit required officers to devote time to the sports and games of the men outside working hours. As

E

bachelors could do this more easily than married men, a proper balance in numbers between the two was desirable, and was generally ensured by the financial obstacle to marriage.

Living in one peace station or another was much the same, and so, as it is proposed to describe life as a bachelor in one, and as a married couple in another, I shall begin with Ferozepore, the first peace station where I stayed for any length of time. In March 1921, after the disbandment of the 3/151st Rifles in Poona, the Dogra company, Roley Ingram-Johnson and I left to join the 38th Dogras at Ferozepore. The battalion had just returned from Egypt, where it had remained after the campaign in Palestine. The 38th was to be my permanent or parent battalion, and looking back I would not have wished otherwise.

Ferozepore just south of the River Sutlej was typical of the south-eastern Punjab. The peasants in the surrounding villages were mostly Sikhs and Muslims, whereas the urban population, as in Ferozepore City, included both these communities and a strong element of Hindus. The country was a featureless plain, and before the summer rains very dry and dusty. The winters were sunny, cold and delightful, but the summers were scorching and exhausting, with temperatures rising to 120°F in the shade.

The garrison of Ferozepore was a varied and well balanced mixture, consisting of :

Brigade Headquarters.
Two Batteries Royal Artillery.
1st Bn. The Welch Regiment.
18th K.G.O. Lancers.
38th Dogras.
14th Punjab Regimental Centre.
Administrative Services.
Ferozepore Arsenal.

Healthy rivalry existed between all units, a fine spirit in the brigade, and heaven help anybody who upset this. The troops could roughly be divided into those who sat on horses, and those who marched on foot. After the First World War and the small wars that followed, the army had been considerably reduced; only the best survived as high standards were set for officers and men, and those who could not attain them faded away. When, on 1 January, all units took part in the annual ceremonial parade, they were a stirring sight, and I felt proud to be a soldier.

Although it was 50 years ago, I clearly remember arriving to join the 38th. The train was met at dawn by a young officer with transport, and we were conveyed to our new home. In the mess the only occupants of the anteroom were two senior majors, Alec Kerr and Bruce Cunningham, Scots and close friends. Both had won the Military Cross, were devoted to the battalion, and for the next ten years played an important part in its life. Bruce used to spend most of his summer leaves hiking in the Dogra country, and was considered the best authority on Dogras in the army. He wrote the Dogra Handbook which all officers serving with Dogras had to study. The two majors gave me a friendly welcome, and made me feel at home straightaway.

Gradually other officers came in to breakfast, and I was introduced to them. The C.O. was Colonel (later Major-General) Henry Barstow, tall, distinguished looking and an outstanding officer. George Renny, who had gone ahead and already joined as second-in-command, seemed very happy to be back with old friends. There were many more officers present than we ever had in the 3/151st, with a higher age and experience level. Due to the disbandment of the extra wartime battalions, regular battalions collected too many officers and some had to be axed.

Contraction of the army meant a reduction in rank and pay for many officers. In the 3/151st I had risen to acting captain and company commander, but had to revert to my substantive rank of lieutenant. Even George Renny dropped to major, until later he succeded Henry Barstow in command. For those with families, having to pay school fees in Britain, reduction in pay came as a serious blow. To give officers some assurance for the future, promotion was put on a time scale, 9 years for captain, 18 for major and 26 for lieutenant-colonel. Before promotion to captain and major, officers had to pass a promotion examination, and before lieutenant-colonel qualify at the Senior Officers' School.

The 38th had a fine team of officers, with a strong element of Scots, who said they were attracted by the Dogras because they were hillmen like themselves. On a guest night when the pipes played reels, and the Scots made us all dance, we might have been a Highland regiment. The team spirit of a battalion is something that cannot be enjoyed outside the Service, and it flourished in the 38th. I can only remember its members with deep affection.

After so long on the frontier it seemed strange to get away from huts and barbed wire, to the bungalows and gardens of Ferozepore. Except for the roofs, residential bungalows all over India were somewhat similar in design. In areas of heavy rainfall the roofs were generally sloping and tiled, but in drier places, like Ferozepore, flat and mud plastered. The walls were usually built of sun-baked bricks, and colour washed inside and out. Good features were the very high ceilings and shady verandahs giving protection from the sun. In rain the flat roofs were apt to leak, and it was advisable to keep buckets handy.

The officers' mess occupied the largest and best of our bungalows, and no effort was spared to make it comfortable and a credit to the battalion. A fighting unit had three scales of mess. The mobile column mess could be loaded on to a few mules, and consisted only of cooking pots, cutlery, enamel mugs and plates; meals were eaten picnic fashion squatting on the ground. The camp mess included the addition of tents and folding furniture. The peace time mess provided all the normal comforts of a permanent home. Packed up during the war, it was now being set up on return of the battalion from overseas, and we all looked forward to a change from austerity.

The anteroom was furnished as a comfortable sitting-room with book cases, periodicals, and a gramophone before the days of radio. The junior subaltern usually had the onerous task of changing records, and longed for the day when somebody more junior would arrive. The walls were reserved for group photographs, portraits of distinguished officers and subedar-majors, and those who had won the highest decorations, all illustrating the history of the battalion with the changes in uniforms and accoutrements.

Normally feeding in the dining-room were six to nine officers, but on guest nights as many as twenty-four. The main feature of the room was the long polished dining table, which was decorated on guest nights with the regimental silver. The walls were covered with hunting trophies such as the heads of tiger, leopard, ibex, urial, markhor and sambhar, the big game of India. It was considered an achievement to bag a head good enough for the mess.

Because of the high cost in India, a billiard table was regarded as a real luxury, but, as the battalion had been on field service for some years with mess funds accumulating, it was decided to buy one in the 38th, and the addition of a billiard room became a major event. Finally there was a separate cardroom, where bridge enthusiasts could play undisturbed; it also provided a refuge for senior officers on turbulent guest nights.

As electricity had not reached Ferozepore, at the beginning of summer, *punkahs* (manually operated fans), were installed in all living rooms. Suspended by ropes from the ceiling a long wooden frame had a skirt attached of heavy cloth, which acted as a fan when swinging. From the frame a rope passed outside over a pulley to the hand of a *punkah-walla* (puller). He did not have a very enviable job, but there was never a shortage of applicants.

Apart from providing a home for the bachelors, and married officers whose wives were away, the mess was the centre of regimental entertainment. Efficiency in a military formation demanded that officers of different units should mix and get to know each other, and in achieving this the mess played an important part. One night a week officers could invite private guests to dinner, and occasionally the battalion entertained official guests or the officers of another unit. At the time we had pipes and drums, and a brass band, which on guest nights played during and after dinner. Those were cheerful occasions, brightened by the mess dress of different regiments, and the uniforms of pipers, bandsmen, mess orderlies and servants.

Ladies only appeared in the mess on rare and special occasions, such as the bachelors' dinner on New Year's Eve. It was customary on Christmas night for married couples to entertain the bachelors, and their hospitality was returned in the mess. After dinner the whole party usually went on to the club to dance in the New Year.

Wherever the British go they take their love of gardening, and most of the bungalows had attractive gardens. In arid country this was quite an expensive luxury, entailing not only the wages of a gardener, but the hire of a man with two bullocks to work a well. Ferozepore Cantonment was well laid out, and in winter the gardens helped to make the place look attractive, but in summer they dried up and the flower beds turned to dust, which lay thick everywhere. The bullocks at the wells struggled to keep some of the lawns and playing fields green until the monsoon rain.

The battalion occupied barracks called Ferozeshah Lines, named after the battle fought nearby against the Sikhs in 1845, when Ferozepore was truly an outpost of the Empire, facing the Sikh kingdom north of the Sutlej. In the First Sikh War, when the Sikhs crossed the river to drive the British out of the Punjab, the garrison of Ferozepore took part in the fierce battles fought in the vicinity.

In Ferozeshah Lines were the offices, administrative buildings, living accommodation and transport lines. Each V.C.O. had a separate dwelling with an enclosed courtyard. Married quarters were provided for a proportion of the men, and those too were walled in for the privacy of *purdah* women. A British officer would not enter the area for inspection without giving notice, so that the women could go inside and not be seen.

Adjoining the barracks were the dusty parade grounds and playing fields, and, beyond, the villages and farmlands in country monotonously flat and somewhat arid. Agriculture depended on irrigation from wells worked by two bullocks or buffaloes turning a Persian wheel, suspended from which a circular chain of earthen pots brought up the water. The wells with their working animals and creaky noise were one of the main features of the Punjab countryside. Disputes over the distribution of water often led to violence, for water meant food.

The work of regimental officers was mostly outdoor training, very enjoyable with Dogras, who were most responsive and enthusiastic. The year was divided into two training seasons, individual in summer and collective in winter. Individual training was mostly confined to the lecture rooms, parade grounds and firing ranges, where a man learnt to handle his weapon and to qualify in firing. He was also taught or brought up to date with all the individual skills of his job, before taking his place in a team. In the summer men also had their annual leave, to ensure maximum attendance in winter for collective training.

This team training was carried out in progressive stages— section, platoon, company and battalion—during which realistic exercises were set for sub-units and their commanders. For the last stage the battalion went into camp for a fortnight, to live and work in field service conditions. Finally manœuvres were held in which many units took part, and two forces opposed each other. The aim was to keep the men and their leaders fit for war, and ready to move to the frontier at short notice.

During individual training and the early stages of collective training, work took place at fixed times, beginning with morning parade, before breakfast in summer to beat the sun, and after breakfast in winter. That was followed by office work, while the men under V.C.O.s attended lectures on training, and school to improve their education which was not high, with some of the men even illiterate. Another parade was carried out in the afternoon, followed by organised games in the evening. In the last stages of collective training we were often out all day on an exercise, and occasionally all night, to compete with which an infantryman had to keep fit, easier in a tropical climate for a subaltern than a middle-aged major.

In most Indian stations professional entertainment did not exist, and therefore a garrison had to rely on its own resources.

For officers the club played a large part in recreation and social life. The Ferozepore Club was typical, providing tennis courts, golf course, cricket and polo grounds, and a club house, which included lounges, cardroom, library, bar and dance hall. If the garrison included a British regiment the club could count on a dance band at moderate cost.

As all the playing fields were on government land, club fees were modest, probably not more than £1 a month. However an impecunious subaltern had to watch his bar bill, especially with a tropical thirst, and the tempting chit or credit system of payment. For those who liked games India was a paradise, and most evenings after parade I played hockey or tennis or rode. In the summer British wives and children went to the hills, so dances were possible only in the winter, and took place once or twice a month. In addition to the wives there were only half a dozen single girls to a hundred bachelors, and the bar used to be packed with surplus males. On occasions the club was used for a regimental ball to celebrate some important anniversary, which would be a grand affair with the men in colourful mess dress, instead of black evening dress.

As hockey was the regimental game I devoted much time to it and managed to get into the battalion team. Only three officers were allowed in the team, and the others were Roley Ingram-Johnson and Henry Power, the Adjutant, who became a close friend. Of the Dogras in the team I remember best Mahantu the tireless centre-half, and Kishan Singh a forward, who later played in the Indian Army team which toured New Zealand. I am glad to say both survived the Second World War and retired as subedars.

Members of the battalion team enjoyed many extra holidays when playing in tournaments. On winning the brigade contest at Ferozepore we went to Lahore for the district contest, and from there to Rawalpindi to play in the command final. Annually we also went to Jhelum for a tournament, which attracted the best teams in the Indian Army. Preparing for those events meant much pleasant team work and hard training, which brought officers in close contact with the men. The tournaments were happy gatherings at which we met old friends from distant stations.

With three mounted units in Ferozepore polo was played regularly, but unlike the wild polo at Dardoni the standard was high, with well bred and properly trained ponies. As I could not afford two ponies I gave up the idea of playing, but kept one pony and took part in all other mounted sports. About Flint I had to make a hard decision; as he was a failure I sold him and bought a stud-bred chestnut mare from an army remount depot. Having learnt a lesson from Flint, this time I made a good choice, and still have some of the silver cups won with Jane in mounted gymkhanas. She was as willing to do her best as Flint was unwilling.

Periodically the mounted units organised amateur races and steeple chases. In addition to riding Jane I was asked to ride the horses of the Nawab of Mamdot, an enormous man and too heavy to jockey. Jane was a good jumper though not fast enough for racing, but I had modest success with the other horses, as the handicappers appreciated that they were built less for speed than for carrying the bulky Nawab.

Unless a subaltern went out shooting it was considered that he lacked some military virtue, so I acquired a shotgun and a sporting rifle. With too many members of the garrison stalking around Ferozepore in search of quail, partridge and duck, the survivors had probably left for safer places, and my expeditions with a shotgun were not fruitful. I therefore decided to try the rifle. My friend Henry Tett from Dardoni had joined the 14th Punjab Centre, and I persuaded him to accompany me on a crocodile shoot. Plans were made with a local *shikari* (shooting guide), who hired a boat, in which we drifted down the River Sutlej for three days. As the weather was dry and hot we took no tent, and slept on the bank at night under the stars.

Because a crocodile hit in the water would disappear, it had to be shot when basking on a sandbank. As can be imagined, crocodiles within fifty miles of the garrison were well acquainted with hunters, very wary, and at the slightest movement slid into the water. The people living along the river regarded these reptiles as enemies, a danger to themselves and their domestic animals, and so we were well received. As we progressed downstream peasants of the riverside villages were only too anxious to point out the favourite sandbanks of the local monsters.

The boat drifted silently in the shadow of either bank, which provided some cover from the vigilant crocodiles, and enabled us to tie up quickly before stalking. If a crocodile was spotted Henry and I would disembark, and begin crawling on our stomachs to get within range. We decided not to bother about any below 9 feet in length, as the sound of a rifle shot would warn any bigger ones that might be ahead. After three days of hard work the final count was four apiece, ranging from 10 to 14 feet.

The white skin of the belly was taken, salted and sent to be tanned and made up. In due course my skins returned in the form of handbags for my mother and sister, and a suitcase which I still have. The best head after curing and mounting I offered to the mess, but it was disdainfully refused. If I wanted to be represented among the *élite* on the dining-room wall, it was suggested that I should go to Kashmir and shoot an ibex, or to the Central Provinces and bag a tiger.

Shooting was good military training for young officers, and greatly encouraged, as it meant roughing it in the open, developing an eye for ground and cover, and skill in using a weapon. Arranging an expedition with itinerary, supplies and transport resembled military planning. Also an officer was brought into close touch with Indian peasants, which increased his understanding of the men who filled the ranks of the army. That was my first contact with rural Punjabis in their own environment, and it was a pleasant relief to meet friendly people after the hostile tribesmen of Waziristan.

The hardiness of the Muslim boatman and *shikari* impressed me, for while we slept on camp beds with mosquito nets, between them and the hard ground was only a rush mat. To keep off the buzzing mosquitoes they pulled a sheet over their heads, which would have suffocated us. They ate only twice a day, a meal of *chappatis* (unleavened wheat pancakes) and curried lentils. Lean, wiry and tireless, they had eyes like hawks, and in the distance could spot the elevated eyes and snout of a croco-dile sticking out of the water, which we had difficulty in seeing with binoculars. No wonder the Punjabis made good, tough soldiers.

Great interest was shown when the Adjutant arranged the summer leave roster. Since sick leave in Mussoorie I had not visited a hill resort, and as the Spartan life on the frontier had given me a reasonable bank balance, I was able to afford a holiday in Kashmir. I planned to spend a fortnight on a trout stream called the Bringhi, a fortnight fishing from a houseboat, and a month playing golf in Gulmarg; the keynote was variety.

The time on the Bringhi was the best part of the holiday, and had the budget permitted I would have stayed longer. Apart from an expensive fishing licence, it involved buying tackle and hiring camp kit, pack-pony transport, *shikari* and cook. The clear rocky stream was in a high beautiful valley, with pine trees coming down to the edge of the water, and after the heat of Ferozepore the air was cool and like champagne. It was my first attempt at fly fishing, but with the aid of a text book, and advice from the expert *shikari*, skill gradually improved. Fried trout was a delicacy never enjoyed on the plains.

The coarse fishing from a boat seemed dull after the Bringhi, and the muddy River Jhelum less attractive than the mountain stream. Every morning and evening I went out in a *shikara* (small boat), to fish for chush, churoo and mahseer, all tasteless as food and only the last a game fighter. The houseboat was a feature of the Kashmir Valley with its river and connecting lakes, provided cheap and comfortable accommodation with simple food, and was well managed by the *manjhi* (boatman) and his team. I often enjoyed a change of scene, when my mobile home was towed or poled along the river and lakes. It was a pleasant form of holiday, but I much preferred the next month in Gulmarg.

Anglers and golfers owed much to the Britons who thought of putting trout in some Kashmir streams, and who discovered and planned Gulmarg. At around 8,500 feet, this beautiful valley is in the high mountains west of Srinagar. The surrounding hills are covered with pine, but the valley has long, open stretches of rich green pasture, rarely seen in India. In the distance appear the towering giants of the Himalayas perpetually covered with snow with Nanga Parbat, the highest, at 26,660 feet. The grassy slopes and rocky streams of the valley provided natural fairways and hazards for two eighteen-hole golf courses, and one nine-hole course for beginners.

Accommodation was available in a few hotels and guest houses, but mostly in rented wooden chalets. The last were ideal for wives and children during the summer, who were joined by husbands when on leave. In most hill resorts emphasis was on social life, but in Gulmarg it was on golf. A round in the morning and another in the afternoon helped a player to recover from the heat down on the plains.

The club house was the main meeting place, though at night Nedou's Hotel was popular for dancing. For the first time I saw a strong contingent of the 'fishing fleet', the name jokingly given to the debutantes, who went out to India to look for husbands. Many were the daughters of officials and soldiers retired in Britain, wishing to follow in their parents' footsteps in India. Drawn to their own kind, the Britons in India seldom married outside their own race, and even without religious prohibitions were as exclusive as the caste Hindus and Muslims.

With an eye to the main object, the 'fishing fleet' did not regard impecunious subalterns as eligible bachelors, and, denied of romance, we had to content ourselves with chasing a golf ball. I spent a delightful month and hoped to see Gulmarg again. From Tangmarg, the motor terminus below Gulmarg, to railhead at Rawalpindi the distance was about 200 miles. The road twisted and turned as it found its way from the mountains to the plains below, and for the greater part followed the course of the fast-flowing River Jhelum. On descending to the plains the country looked parched, the heat was oppressive, and the mosquitoes began to bite. I did not relish a return to the *punkahs*, but looked forward to seeing Jane, and felt sorry that she had not enjoyed the green grass and cool of Gulmarg.

The Indian Army was reorganised in 1922. The four Dogra

battalions, the 37th, 38th, 41st and 2/41st, were grouped in one regiment, and renamed respectively 1st (Prince of Wales Own), 2nd, 3rd and 10th Battalion 17th Dogra Regiment. A close link was maintained between all battalions, and officers in turn served for a time with the 10th at Jullundur, which acted as the Regimental Centre and trained recruits for the other three active battalions.

In 1924 the 2nd Battalion left Ferozepore and for the next ten years followed the trail-Tank, Manzai (frontier), Bombay, Deolali, Rawalpindi, Khajuri Plain (frontier) and Razmak (frontier). At the end of that period Lt.-Colonel Maurice Bickford was in command; he was an experienced mountaineer, who was in his element on the frontier hills.

* * *

When Elsa and I married in 1934, we had a short spell together in England, and a pleasant voyage in the P. & O. liner *Rawal-pindi*. The snags for a service wife soon became evident, for then I had to leave her in an hotel in Murree, and rejoin the battalion at Razmak, a non-family station. Having waited longer than most to marry, I was already a temporary widower. However, we were due to move to a peace station in six months, and after fifteen years of mess life I looked forward to my own home. Our destination turned out to be Kamptee in the Central Provinces, and we moved there in November.

A British garrison was established at Kamptee in 1821 after the Mahratta Wars, to ensure law and order in the large city of Nagpur and surrounding country. Many ruins showed that the cantonment had been larger and more important, before the British frontier was pushed northwards. The garrison had since been reduced to two battalions, one British and one Indian. Our neighbours were first the York and Lancaster Regiment, and then the King's Shropshire Light Infantry.

Kamptee had a bad reputation for health, and for this reason was an unpopular station, particularly with British troops. The winter lasted for only three months, and was not really cold, with no need for fires. The long summer was made bearable only by the monsoon from June to October, but though that lowered the temperature it increased humidity and insects, notably malarial mosquitoes. It also drove snakes out of their water-logged holes, and at night it was unwise to move without a light.

We were allotted a bungalow on a high bank of the River Kanhan. Most of the bungalows had tiled roofs, but ours had a thick thatch, which not only improved its appearance, but provided excellent shelter from the vertical rays of the sun. Petworth, as it was named, will always be remembered as our first home.

Furnishing Petworth gave us great pleasure. My bachelor possessions contributed only a few Persian rugs, but in England we had acquired a barrel full of glass and crockery, a canteen of cutlery, blankets, linen and some useful wedding presents. Furniture was hired from the bazaar and arrived in four bullock carts. All the earthen floors had to be covered with *chattai* (palm frond) matting, which was woven on the spot by two experts, and, lastly a *durzi* (tailor) made up curtains and chair covers, squatting on the floor with his sewing machine. The old mud bungalow looked quite transformed, and we were well pleased with our efforts. As the only servant brought with us was bearer Feroz Din, others had to be engaged locally, of whom the most important was Jaggu the cook. He proudly informed Elsa that he could produce 52 kinds of sweet dessert, but we did not try them all! We were ready for our first house-warming.

Tulsi, my soldier orderly, regarded himself as being superior to the servants and kept them in place. In Razmak he had acted as my batman, and on operations as my runner, delivering written and verbal messages. In a peace station orderlies could not be used as domestic servants, but a point was stretched in letting them look after a car, and our Wolseley became his main hobby. He was defeated by the names of car parts and invented his own, which I had to learn; he made full use of his military vocabulary, for instance the carburettor was called the headquarters.

Jane had died and been replaced by Kate, an Australian mare

and the best pony I ever possessed. Brownie, an Alsatian bitch, completed the family, and gave us much pleasure. She was an incurable hunter and gave the squirrels in the garden no peace, but fortunately could not climb trees.

With winter ahead we could look forward to three perfect months; a change from the monastic life of Razmak. The social obligations of a married man proved far greater than those of a bachelor. By tradition all married couples and bachelors in the battalion were dined at least once a year, and also many friends outside the regiment were entertained. As nearby Nagpur was the capital of the province, the Governor and a fair number of Civil Service, Police, and Forest officials lived there. The Governor, Sir Hyde Gowan, was an enthusiastic tennis player, and occasionally invited us to his enjoyable tennis parties. The Government House ball was the social event of the year, and a bright scene with colourful dresses and *saris*, different mess uniforms and the elaborate attire of Indian princes.

With only two units in the station the club was much smaller than usual, yet provided a lounge, bar, small ballroom, tennis and squash courts. With not enough members for regular dances, these were held on rare occasions, augmented by the civil colony from Nagpur. Once the battalion gave a regimental ball at the club in such grand style that it took the mess fund years to recover.

Riding was our favourite recreation in Kamptee, especially during the monsoon when the ground was too wet for games. Elsa had not ridden previously, but soon became very proficient. Most mornings when I was on parade she would hack Kate with Brownie trotting alongside, and we would meet for breakfast with tropical thirsts, assuaged by endless cups of tea or iced coffee. In the evenings we often rode together on Kate and a borrowed horse. Somebody was always on leave or on a course, and only too glad to have his horse exercised, though some years later we managed to own a second horse.

Since the battalion had left Ferozepore, Colonels Barstow, Renny, Kerr and Cunningham had commanded and retired, and at Kamptee Maurice Bickford was succeeded as C.O. by Lt.-

Colonel Harold Andrews. Ian Dewar, who had followed me as Adjutant was relieved by John Cruddas. I clearly remember Ian's joy, when his unusually long term ended as junior subaltern. He met his successor at the railway station and took great care of him, keeping the surprise until after dinner, when he firmly led him to the gramophone and said, "I have played this damned instrument for two years, and now have much pleasure in handing it over to you". Most popular with officers and men, Ian was killed in action by Mahsuds, when serving with the South Waziristan Scouts.

New subalterns caused a certain amount of interest, but brides caused a far greater stir; all would be agog to see whom Bill or Harry had married. As an honour, during her first year, a bride took precedence over the other ladies on formal occasions, such as a mixed dinner party in the mess, at which she sat on the C.O's right.

We were now located in what the army called the sloth belt of India, where it was difficult to keep the men and ourselves fit. It was impossible to maintain the standard of invigorating Razmak, but we did our best. Apart from the trying climate, except for a few months in the year, malaria was very prevalent; the prophylactics used in the Second World War had yet to be discovered. After a severe attack of malaria it was difficult to pick up in the heat of summer.

The C.O's recipe for fitness was a route march every Saturday morning, which, normally of about ten miles, was increased to fifteen or twenty as the manœuvre season approached. Infantrymen were useless who could not march long distances carrying arms and equipment, and those marches ensured that we could. Manœuvres were held in winter near Laknadon, located between Kamptee and Jubbulpore, which had a large garrison. Each of the last two places fielded a force, and the two opposed each other in an annual mock battle in country which was hilly and wooded, and a pleasant change from the flat monotonous plains of North India to which we were accustomed.

The jungles of Central India were famous for big game, and attracted hunters from all over India. Instead of spending their summer holidays in hill resorts, they journeyed to hot jungles in pursuit of tiger, leopard, the big sambhar deer and other game. Being unable to resist the cool air of the mountains I had never done this, but now it was different; the jungle was at our front door. Elsa and I were attracted by the forest and wild animals and often ventured out. It was easier to work in pairs and share expenses, which we generally did with Captain Edward Saw, and benefited from his experience and good company.

The forests were carefully preserved, and the shooting of wild animals controlled by the Forest Service. The only habitations were very occasional hamlets or small villages of primitive jungle folk, who provided labour in the forest, tilled their fields and grazed cattle. To assist the Forest Officer in his work each large block of forest had a small furnished resthouse, in which he could stay during his visits. Those houses were usually situated near a hamlet, and could be rented by hunters.

About sixty miles from Kamptee and twenty off the main road to Jubbulpore, we discovered a most delightful place called Kandlai, with a resthouse on a low hill overlooking the small River Pench. To avoid being crowded out we kept it a dark secret, and spent many happy weekends at Kandlai, and also a few days at Christmas. The resthouse saved us from taking tents and camp furniture, but food, cooking pots, china, cutlery, bedding, weapons, fishing tackle, servant and dog, all had to be loaded on a small car. It went well on the main road, but on the jungle track often required manual assistance.

The chief joy of Kandlai was the attractive stream, bordered by the forest and containing large rocks of white marble. The pleasures the place provided were swimming, fishing, and observation of the wild creatures coming down to drink, such as deer, peacocks and always large grey monkeys. Most of the animals were nocturnal, and to see them meant rising in the dark and setting off for the area to be watched. In the half light of dawn the sambhar, nilgai and spotted cheetal deer could be seen returning to their sleeping quarters. Fishing was best in the evening, and with fine trout tackle landing mahseer weighing up to ten pounds provided excellent sport.

F

With deer and wild pig I had some success, and at last bagged a sambhar head good enough for the mess, but the real trophies, tiger and leopard, eluded me. The few around Kandlai seemed very wily, and to defeat them needed prolonged organisation, not possible during a weekend. The poor man's method was to buy one or two goats or young buffaloes, tether them in the jungle and wait for a kill, which might take days, and then keep watch over the body. The raja or rich man did it more easily with enormous beats, and himself on an elephant.

Fleetingly I saw a leopard on a few occasions, and twice a tiger. On a Christmas shoot we found a sambhar doe, which had only just been killed by a tiger. John Cruddas and I sat near the kill to keep scavengers away, while the *shikaris* went off to get material for a *machan* (a platform tied in a tree for sitting over a kill). We were sitting with our backs to a tree, resting, when a large head appeared in the bushes only twenty yards away. The tiger peered at us and at his breakfast, and appeared to be sizing up the situation. As tigers are not supposed to return in daylight, we were caught unawares with our rifles not at the ready, and by the time we raised them the tiger had vanished. John sat up all night but the tiger did not return, and so must have taken fright, or killed again and satisfied his hunger.

On another occasion, after a dawn walk, the *shikari* and I were sitting on a ridge admiring the sunrise, when thirty yards away in a bamboo thicket, we suddenly heard the frightened squeals of a cornered pig, and the low growls of a tiger. Very cautiously I approached the bamboo, which must have distracted the tiger, and saved the pig, because he shot out of the thicket for dear life. We did not see the tiger, but from the jungle noises knew he was moving away from us towards a hamlet. From his pug marks, and the alarm calls of monkeys and deer there was no difficulty in following. It was strange that he should head for the hamlet in broad daylight, but the reason became clear; he was very hungry.

We reached the hamlet to find great commotion, for Master Stripes had just killed a cow. On that occasion it was my turn to sit up all night. This is an uncomfortable, tiring pastime, and, despite insect repellent on hands and face, mosquitoes and biting ants always find unprotected parts of the body. The discomfort might be worth a tiger skin, but I did not get mine. On occasions I heard an animal tearing at the kill, but when I raised my rifle, and switched on the torch strapped to it, the light revealed a jackal or civet cat. Once I heard the tiger moaning near by, but with my outline showing against the stars his fear proved greater than his hunger and he kept away.

My last encounter with a tiger also failed. Determined to get a tiger, Edward Saw looked beyond Kandlai, and discovered Sakata, a very thickly wooded and hilly block reputed to have a few. As usual we went out for a weekend and put out a buffalo, which was killed the first night, and the body dragged into very thick undergrowth, where the remains were presumably being guarded by the tiger. Where the undergrowth was not so dense, two *machans* were set up forty yards apart for Edward and myself, and a beat arranged. As Elsa was very depressed at being left behind, at the last minute I agreed to her sitting in my *machan*, against the advice of all the text books.

So as not to startle the tiger, the beaters talked naturally and occasionally tapped a tree, as if they were woodcutters going to work. As they had to drive the tiger several hundred yards through dense jungle, I thought the chance of seeing him very slight, but suddenly he appeared in the bushes coming straight towards us. I decided to wait for a closer and clearer shot, when Elsa spotted him, and in a stage whisper said ,"There he is", and pointed her camera. It was enough for Stripes, who vanished like a flash. How right the text books were about not taking the girl friend, but Elsa says the memory is worth more than a moulting skin. The beautiful sambhar and cheetal deer must have shared my disappointment, for the tiger would continue to gobble one of them every week.

Elsa sometimes accompanied me on dawn walks, and once we were rewarded by an unusual experience. Ahead we heard the barking of wild dogs, so leaving her and the *shikari* I crept forward, and on arriving at the edge of a deep *nallah*, found standing in the middle of a pool a graceful golden samhar doe.

Round the pool were several wild dogs with large batlike ears, of which I shot one and the rest vanished. The *shikari* and I waded into the water and pulled out the doe, which was unhurt, but too terrified to leave us. Though quite wild it recognised friends, and stood trembling while we patted it. We had great difficulty in persuading it to leave us, but at last it trotted away into the jungle. A pack of wild dogs will clear a jungle block of deer quicker than any other predators.

Our visits to the jungle also had a human value, for they brought us into contact with the short, dark, primitive jungle folk, who knew the jungle intimately, and were as much at home in it as the sambhar and tiger. They were very friendly, and always ready to act as *shikaris* or beaters, which meant remuneration, and, when we shot a stag or a wild boar, a feast; with tom-tomming until the early hours.

The three winter months passed too quickly, and when faced with the long hot summer, most of the wives, especially those with children, departed to the hills, but a few, including Elsa, decided to endure the heat until their husband's turn for two months' leave. There had been progress since Ferozepore, and we were greatly helped with electricity and fans. Also available was a wonderful local invention called a *kuskus-tatti*, consisting of rush fibres tied thickly on to bamboo frames, which were fitted to open doors and windows. During the heat of the day these spongy screens were kept soaked with water. Hot dry air striking the screens made them cold by rapid evaporation, which in turn lowered the temperature in the rooms. This worked only in the dry season, and when the monsoon began in June the screens were removed.

At night in the dry summer season we slept outside, some distance from the bungalow, which radiated heat. The hot ground was sprayed with water to lower the temperature, and an electric fan placed at the foot of the beds, but still, in the intense heat, it was often impossible to sleep restfully. Being outside we were also disturbed by noises such as dogs barking, jackals howling and flying foxes, or large bats, squeaking. The bats arrived in swarms to eat wild figs, of which we had a few trees in the garden. By my bed I kept a loaded shotgun, because shooting was the only way to frighten the bats away and to get any relief from their hideous noise. It was easier to sleep during the monsoon, as the cool rain sheeting down lowered the temperature, but even then we slept on the verandah, for it was too hot inside.

In these conditions summer leave came as a great relief. From Kamptee the hill resorts of the Himalayas in the north and of the Nilgiris in the south were about the same distance. For a change we decided to visit the south, and for two years in succession went to Kotagiri in the Nilgiri Hills. The train journey via Madras took a day and a half, and was extremely hot and uncomfortable; by day the metal parts of the carriage were too hot to touch. As a precaution against heatstroke the practice was to buy ice by the hundredweight, and fill a tub in the middle of the compartment. In it were also put dozens of bottles of mineral water; ordinary water not being safe to drink. The ice reduced the temperature in the compartment a few degrees and kept the drinks cold, but, melting rapidly, needed frequent replenishment. The last stage of the journey from the sweltering plains to over 6,000 feet, with the air rapidly getting cooler, seemed like deliverance from hell.

The Nilgiri Hills were on a smaller scale than the giant mountains of the Himalayas, but most attractive with a great variety of trees. Some of the slopes were used for cultivating tea, and tea bushes grown under shady trees added to the beauty of the scenery. Four hill resorts existed within a short motor drive of each other, Ootacamund, Conoor, Wellington and Kotagiri, which were very popular with Europeans in South India, and a fair number settled there on retirement.

Kotagiri was the smallest of these resorts, with only one hotel, the Blue Mountain, where we stayed. For us the chief attraction was a delightful nine-hole golf course, on which we played most days. Unlike those of a military garrison, people there came from many walks of life, and it was a change to meet others with a variety of experience. Dick Millward, a local tea planter, kindly invited us to spend a few days on his tea garden, and it was interesting to compare his life with ours. Like a soldier he enjoyed an outdoor life, but with a more settled home, and in the Nilgiris a much healthier climate.

As in Kashmir a few of the higher, cooler streams in the Nilgiris had been stocked with trout, and I enjoyed fishing in peaceful green valleys that reminded me of England. Compared with Kashmir the streams were smaller, and so were the trout, but offered excellent sport and were very edible.

Having enjoyed our two months in Kotagiri so much, we returned the following summer, but for a change rented a small holiday cottage overlooking the golf course. Several furnished holiday cottages were available, and including a few servants cost no more than hotel accommodation, yet in some ways provided greater comfort and privacy.

Luckily we did not have to face a third summer in Kamptee, as my turn came for eight months' home leave. Once again our possessions were packed in numerous cases with tobacco and neem leaves to discourage white ants, and moved to the absent officers' store. During our leave the battalion was ordered to the frontier for operations, and, as mentioned in the previous chapter, we had to cut short our holiday and return. We travelled to Peshawar together, where I left Elsa in an hotel, and her second arrival in India, like the first, was followed by a separation.

In December, on completing its mission, the battalion returned to Kamptee, a journey taking four days by troop train, and as wives were allowed to travel on the train, Elsa joined at Rawalpindi. The long train carried about six hundred men, sixty horses and mules, field service stores and tents. Troop trains were notoriously slow for two reasons : time spent in sidings to avoid interfering with regular schedules; halts for meals, cooked in kitchen cars and eaten in sidings. However, with the discomforts of Waziristan behind us, and the prospect of Christmas in Kamptee, spirits were high. At some of the long halts we went along to the horse wagon to cheer Kate and the other horses with lumps of sugar. Brownie shared our two berth compartment, and so the family was complete.

Life in Kamptee soon returned to normal. The trip to Waziristan had done the men good, and they were looking much fitter. Edward, Elsa and I continued to visit our old haunt Kandlai, walk the jungle at dawn, and catch mahseer among the marble rocks. All were determined to make the most of the short winter before the dreaded summer; but from another summer in Kamptee Elsa and I were spared.

In May 1938, as a junior major, I was appointed to command 11th Bn. 17th Dogra Regiment (Indian Territorial Force) based on Jullundur. Like British Territorial units its members were not regular, full-time soldiers, but civilians who assembled only for periodic training. The prospect of a change and an independent command was most acceptable. That it entailed much touring in the Dogra country was an added attraction, for though I knew Dogras as soldiers, I had seen little of their country and home background. Now it would be possible to do this.

On that occasion we had been settled for only four months, when the packing cases were again brought out. Of the servants only Feroz Din accompanied us, as his home was north in Poonch, whereas the others were all locals with no desire to leave. Tulsi, the orderly, presented a worrying problem, as he pleaded to go with us. I very much wanted to take him, and it would have been simple to transfer him to the small regular staff of the 11th. I discussed the matter with the C.O., but he refused emphatically on the grounds that an orderly was a soldier, and not a private retainer. Tulsi felt he was being deserted and took it very badly, as his simple mind understood loyalty, but not the niceties of British red tape.

The sequel was even more harrowing. I did not see Tulsi again until seven years later, when we liberated prisoners of the Japanese in Singapore. I entered their ghastly camp looking for 2nd Battalion Dogras, to find Tulsi looking starved and gaunt. I expressed my delight at seeing him alive, but he shattered me by saying, "Sahib this would not have happened if you had taken me with you". I tried to cheer him up by replying, "At least you are alive Tulsi and will see your family; with me you might have been killed". Unfortunately he had brooded too long over a grievance, which I could not set right.

On saying good-bye to the 2nd Dogras at Kamptee, I had expected to rejoin them after three years with the 11th Battalion, but by then events had taken a very unexpected turn, for the following year the war began, and in Malaya all the 2nd were made prisoners.

CHAPTER IV

THE DOGRAS

The Dogras inhabit the foothills of the Himalayas, roughly between the rivers Chenab and Sutlej. They derive their name from Durgara, which was the ancient name of the western part of their country, now called Jammu. Dogras claim descent from the Aryan invaders of India, who came from the region of the Oxus, and settled in the Punjab about the fifteenth century B.C. Judged by their relatively fair complexions and western features, they are probably of purer Aryan descent than any other race in India. This applies more to the higher castes, the Brahmans and Rajputs, who, by strict marriage laws, have resisted integration with the original dark skinned inhabitants, the Dravidians. Despite centuries of Muslim persecution Dogras had refused to be converted to Islam, and remained true to their Hindu religion.*

Mahmud became Sultan of Ghazni in A.D. 997, and soon began a series of raids deep into India. His aims were to plunder, collect slaves and kill idolators, all of which he achieved with ruthless brutality. Those raids were the beginning of the Muslim invasions, and the bitter resistance by the Hindus to save themselves and their religion.

* See map, page 144.

In 1001, near Peshawar, on his second expedition, Mahmud of Ghazni defeated the Rajputs under Raja Jaipal, who committed suicide rather than face disgrace. Jaipal was succeeded at Lahore by his son Raja Anandpal, who returned to the attack a few years later, together with forces of the Rajas of Delhi, Ajmer, Gwalior, Ujjain, Kanauj and Jullundur; the last a Dogra kingdom at that time. After forty days of battle the Hindu Rajputs had all but conquered, when the elephant of Anandpal became uncontrollable, turned and fled. The Rajputs took that as a signal for retreat, and Mahmud gained such a complete victory that he was able to occupy the Punjab. In 1009 he stormed and sacked the famous fort and temple of Kangra, in the very heart of the Dogra country.

The Jullundur contingent, which marched to meet Mahmud, was composed of Dogra Rajputs, ancestors of soldiers of the Dogra Regiment. Centuries of Muslim invasion and persecution have never been forgotten or forgiven, and explain the conflict and massacres of 1947, when British rule ended. During the Raj no soldiers were more responsive in defending the north-west frontier than the Dogras; for them, it was a personal affair.

The Muslim invasions were carried out with the utmost savagery. Fanatical marauders sacked the luxurious cities of Lahore, Delhi and the Ganges plain, yelling for God and the Prophet, but seeking only women and plunder. The rajas and their Rajput retainers manned the walls of their fortresses, while the people flocked to the temples, where the Brahmans performed their sacrifices and implored the gods for succour. The hardy Muslims would burst through the gates, or scale the walls in overwhelming numbers, to crush the Rajputs, who fought with courage and desperation. When the battle ended the licentious ruffians would head for the *zenanas*, throw down the temples, profane the gods, and carry off the plunder with young men and maidens to sell as slaves in Kabul and Ghazni.

The natural route for the invaders was the plain of the Punjab, Jumna and Ganges, stretching from Peshawar to Calcutta, and easily traversed by men and horses. Also, as it was the most fertile part of India, it provided all the needs of an army living on the country. There too were rich cities and villages with prospects of plunder. After the Muslims had conquered that northern plain, they extended their rule to the south, where the State of Hyderbad, ruled by a Muslin Nizam, was a relic of their southern invasion.

The Rajputs of the Punjab, refusing to submit, withdrew north and south to areas less accessible and easier to defend. The northern group, the Dogras, fell back to the mountains and foot-hills of the Himalayas. The southern group retreated towards the Indus Desert, to a region named after themselves, Rajputana, now Rajasthan.

Though ousted by the Muslim invaders from the hill tracts west of the River Chenab, east of the river the Rajputs success-fully held out. The rugged hills and forests provided conceal-ment, and idea positions for defence and ambush. If hard pressed the Hindus withdrew deeper into the mountains, leaving little to plunder. The invaders tended to avoid the hazards of the hills and to keep to the plains, where they could move easily and with greater security.

Defensive battles in the foothills of the Himalayas, and in Rajputana, however, fell far short of defeating the invaders at the frontier, or of throwing them out of India, which the Hindus failed to do, despite the courage of their Rajput soldiers. With the advantage of fighting on their own home ground, it is interest-ing to consider the reasons for their failure.

Anyone from a temperate region, after enduring a few sum-mers in India, might be inclined to attribute the failure of the Hindus to the debilitating climate. Perhaps men in the tropics are not a match for more vigorous men from colder climates, but this notion is refuted by the success of the Sikhs, at the end of the eighteenth and beginning of the nineteenth centuries. Under their most famous Maharaja, Ranjit Singh, they decisively de-feated the Muslims, and, by 1834, ruled not only the Punjab, but across the Indus to Peshawar.

During the British Raj, the Rajputs showed, in battles against the Pathans, Germans, Turks and Japanese, that they were second to none as warriors. That their ancestors allowed India to be conquered by Muslims, must have been due to some weakness in the Hindu system. According to caste only a small *élite* had the honour and privilege to bear arms. That enabled the rajas, with their Rajput retainers, to battle among themselves, and to keep down the lower castes; but, against a powerful invader, the system failed to utilise the potential strength of the Hindus.

After many centuries of oppression the military weakness of caste was recognised and eliminated by a section of the Hindus, who broke with tradition and founded a new religion. The rebels were the Sikhs of the Punjab. Though the movement was founded as a peaceful sect by the first Guru or prophet Nanak (1469–1539), it was developed into a militant, religious brotherhood by the tenth and last Guru, Gobind Singh (1675–1708). When, at the age of eleven, the Muslims presented him with his father's head, they made their bitterest enemy.

The new order was based on steel or the *kirpan* (holy sword), an appropriate answer to the Middle East scimitar which had conquered India. The Sikhs repudiated idolatry, and worshipped one God according to the scriptures of their holy book, the Granth Sahib. Caste was abolished and all Sikhs were made equal in the eyes of God, and given the solemn duty of crushing the hated Muslims.

A soldier requires a distinctive uniform to make him feel part of a military organisation. The Sikhs identified themselves by wearing or carrying the five Ks: *kesh*, unshorn hair and beard; *kungha*, comb in the hair; *kuchcha*, shorts instead of the feminine Hindu *dhoti* or loin cloth; *kara*, steel bangle on the right wrist; *kirpan*, sword. They banded themselves into an army called the Khalsa or Pure, and in their daily prayer said, "First of all I worship thee, O Sword".

All this sounds rather theatrical, but the results were very real. At long last the Sikhs not only threw off Muslim rule in the Punjab, but extended their own dominion up to the foot of the Afghan hills. Then they missed a great opportunity, for after defeating the Muslims had they acted with justice and humanity, they might have altered the course of history in India. Unfortunately the Sikhs proved as tyrannical as the Muslims. Their system of government remained the same, durbar rule, with ruthless soldiers extracting tribute for the palace and themselves.

The Sikh kingdom stretching from the Sutlej to the northwest frontier was the creation of Maharaja Ranjit Singh, who ruled at Lahore from 1799 to 1839. The many vassal states, which it included, were held together by the dominating personality of Ranjit Singh, and fear of the Khalsa. He was succeeded by his only legitimate son Kharak Singh who was murdered, and then by a reputed son Sher Singh, who suffered the same fate. Finally in 1843, another reputed son, the boy Dalip Singh, was placed on the throne, with his mother Rani Jindon as Regent. Without stability at the centre the Sikh kingdom began to collapse, and the Punjab was thrown into confusion and anarchy.

The Khalsa became mutinous and difficult to control, and to divert its energies was launched against the British south of the Sutlej; thus began the First Sikh War. The war ended with a British victory, but only after severe fighting and heavy losses on both sides. The British were anxious to revive the Sikh kingdom, and appointed Sir Henry Lawrence as resident at Lahore to help with its reconstruction. His views on reforms, however, were not acceptable to the Sikh chiefs with vested interests, and brought about the Second Sikh War.

After the defeat of the Sikhs, in 1849, it was decided to annex the Punjab. Considering its large martial population, and the few British troops available, that bold step succeeded only because it had the support of the people, who had suffered enough from tyranny and incompetence, whether from Muslim, Sikh or Hindu rulers. The Punjabis were prepared to give the British a trial, and encouraged them to stay a hundred years. Peasants immediately enlisted in the British forces, and none with more enthusiasm than the Dogras.

The Dogra country can be divided roughly into the western region between the rivers Chenab and Ravi, and the eastern region between the Ravi and Sutlej. Mountains and hills provide natural barriers, and before being linked by roads and railways the Dogras tended to divide into clans, each determined to manage its own affairs in its own valley, or group of valleys; that clan spirit was very noticeable in the regiment. For centuries the Dogra country was divided into small states, each under its own raja, but, following constant tribal wars, boundaries often changed, or whole states were absorbed by their neighbours.

Realising that disunity had been the chief weakness of the Dogras against their common foes, who were first the Muslims and then the Sikhs, Raja Gulab Singh of Jammu began to consolidate the western region. An outstanding Dogra, he achieved what seemed the impossible, and, before British annexation of the Punjab, had extended his rule over most of Jammu. In contrast the eastern region remained divided into many small states. The rajas of both regions had been made tributaries of Maharaja Ranjit Singh.

In constant conflict the Dogras had survived only by their hardiness and courage, though at times they had no choice but to meet the capricious demands of the Muslims and Sikhs. If they failed to do so, rapacious and plundering armies were let loose to teach a bloody lesson and to gather loot. After independence in 1947, I witnessed a return to this kind of savagery, as described in later chapters. No wonder that a century previously, a few thousand British soldiers, and a few dozen administrators, had been welcomed to the Punjab, except by the tyrants.

Paying tribute to the Sikh Durbar and their own rajas imposed a heavy burden on the Dogras, as tax collecting was done by unscrupulous ruffians, who left little behind. The menace to life and property in the hills ended only with the annexation of the Punjab after the Second Sikh War (1848–49).

During the First Sikh War (1845–46) Raja Gulab Singh, anxious to throw off the yoke of the Sikhs, evaded taking the field on their side. Appreciating his neutrality, after the war the British allowed him to extend his rule over Muslim Kashmir, which had been ceded by the Sikhs. For handing over a country they hardly knew to the Dogras, the British have never been forgiven by the Muslims. Equally the British offended the Hindus by supporting the continuance of Muslim rule in the predominantly Hindu State of Hyderabad. After independence India annexed Hyderabad by force, but three wars between India and Pakistan have failed to end the dispute over Kashmir. At the time of the Indian Mutiny, in gratitude for freedom from the Sikhs, Gulab Singh remained loyal to the British, and sent a contingent of Dogras to help in the siege of Delhi, where it rendered excellent service.

On annexing the Punjab the British proceeded to establish law, order and just administration, as done in other provinces. Finally that policy resulted in the British administering about two-thirds of India, and in princes continuing with British guidance, to rule the rest comprising about 560 states. In the western Dogra region, Jammu, and in the eastern region, Chamba, Mandi, Suket and Bilaspur continued as princely states. Other parts of both regions were taken over and included in the British administered districts of Sialkot, Gurdaspur, Kangra and Hoshiarpur. Many tiny states were abolished, where a separate administration was uneconomical and inefficient.

The eastern region, where Dogras greatly outnumbered Muslims, exceeded the western region in area and population. Although the western region had a strong element of Dogras, the population was mainly Muslim. The Jammu Dogras were heavily recruited for the army and police of the State of Jammu and Kashmir, which reduced the number available for the Indian Army. With fewer Dogras in the west, and the attraction there of State service, the eastern region provided about three-quarters of the Dogras in the Indian Army.

When Dogra soldiers discussed the merits of the Raj they usually summed up by saying that the British had brought justice and security to India, and so had their support. For centuries their ancestors had suffered from violence and tyranny, but now people could leave their homes without fear, knowing that their families were safe. The loyalty of the Dogra soldier to his British officer was based on these beliefs, and the fact that both men liked and respected each other. The life of a Dogra very much revolved around his religion, and to gain his confidence an officer had to give full consideration to his religious belief and customs.

A Christian can express his religion briefly in the words of Christ, "Love the Lord thy God" and "Love thy neighbour as thyself" (*St. Mark* 12 : 30–31). A Muslim too can describe his faith in a few words : there is one God, Allah, and Mohammed is his Prophet. For a Dogra the explanation of Hinduism is more complex. Although Dogras were willing to talk about their religion, theologians among them were rare, and discussions tended to be very limited. I can, therefore, only describe Hinduism in its simplest form, as understood and observed by Dogra soldiers.

The religion brought by the Aryans into India from Central Asia was a form of nature worship, the deities of the early Hindus being Surya, Agni and Indra, or sun, fire and rain. The beliefs of that primitive period, and the manner of praising and invoking the gods, are contained in the hymns and texts of the ancient Vedas. Gradually a special priesthood evolved, who officiated at ceremonies and sacrifices, and became devoted to religious meditation. As their experience led them to believe that beyond material things there must be an all pervading power or spirit, Surya, Agni and Indra gave way to a new trinity, Brahma the creator, Vishnu the preserver and Siva the destroyer, jointly known as Parmatma or God.

The priesthood named Brahmans, after Brahma, became a sacred and all powerful order, as only they could mediate between the Gods and humanity. They invented elaborate rituals, which still govern the lives of Hindus, and in which only Brahmans can officiate. The complexity of Hinduism is perhaps explained by its Brahman origin. While Christianity, Islam and Buddhism were each founded on the teaching of one man, Hinduism endeavoured to embody the varying views of a wide priesthood.

In order to maintain their favoured position the Brahmans made the priesthood hereditary, and thus established the caste system, by which every man's status in life is decided by his birth. The main classification became :

(a) *Brahman:* priests, advisers, ministers.
(b) *Kshatriya* or *Rajput:* those of royal descent; rajas, governors, warriors, landlords.
(c) *Vaisiya:* traders, artisans, cultivators, herdsmen.
(d) *Sudra:* menial workers; mostly the conquered aborigines.

In course of time these main groups were subdivided into castes, based on hereditary occupation. Segregation of the castes was maintained by strict marriage laws, and a marriage outside the caste limits meant degrading the whole family.

With Dogra Rajputs I have often discussed the caste system, and their attitude was always quite uncompromising, for without caste they maintained that discipline would break down, and village organisation be destroyed. As through caste every man was assigned his occupation by God, he had a duty to keep to it. The system has survived for a few thousand years, enforced by those at the top, the Brahmans and Rajputs, whom it most benefits. In a modern world those at the bottom, compelled to do the menial and dirty jobs, are becoming restive.

Christianity has its saints, who are remembered for their pious and dedicated lives. Hinduism too has its historial and legendary heroes and heroines, but goes a step further by elevating them to the status of minor gods. The omnipotent God is considered to be so remote, that he must be approached through these intermediary gods, who are more human and approachable. There are many of these, and communities and regions worship those with whom they are traditionally linked.

Images of these gods are placed in Hindu temples, but towards them there are two schools of thought. Some, generally the educated, regard them only as symbols to concentrate the mind, and to help prayer to the spirit beyond. Others, mostly the uneducated, worship the idol itself, believing that in it dwells the spirit of the god. In general conversation I rarely heard Dogras refer to the minor gods, but often, like Muslims, to the Almighty. Thus a Dogra would say, "Thanks to the Parmatma we have had a good harvest". Yet when praying for a good harvest he probably went to the temple, and prayed to Durga, the favourite goddess of the Dogras, symbol of hope, strength, power and victory in war.

Hindus have great veneration for cattle, which are regarded as sacred, and regard nothing more repugnant than the killing and eating of a cow, the animal on whose milk man is reared. In 1934, in the frontier camp of Razmak, an incident occurred, showing the intense feelings of Hindus on the slaughter of cattle. A Hindu gate sentry was so upset at seeing cattle being taken out for slaughter, that he shot dead the two Muslim herdsmen. At the court-martial of the sentry for murder, during which I acted as interpreter, the defence maintained that he had been provoked by the sight of slaughter cattle, and his religious feelings deeply hurt.

Hinduism puts much emphasis on the strict observance of rituals and ceremonies. Whereas for Christians religious ceremonies of a personal nature take place in church, for Hindus they are generally performed in the home. There are numerous personal ceremonies ranging through birth, investiture with the sacred thread, marriage and death. Lasting for many days, with the attendance of Brahmans, and the feeding of friends and relations, they impose a heavy burden on the poor, who often incur crippling debts rather than fail in their obligations. Dogra soldiers always endeavoured to arrange their home leave to coincide with these ceremonies.

Apart from the personal ceremonies Hindus celebrate many religious festivals, which appear to be merry occasions with much feasting, music and singing. Providing so much enjoyment, the festivals are one of the attractions of the Hindu religion.

Every Dogra battalion had its *mandir* (temple), and a Brahman priest or Pandit. To allow for constant changes of units, all permanent barracks had a Hindu *mandir*, Sikh *gurdwara* and Muslim mosque. When moving, the battalion took its idol, furnishings and holy books, so that in a place like a frontier camp, a makeshift temple could be set up in a hut or tent. From my experience the Pandit and the temple played a very wholesome part in the life of a battalion, and the strict code of

G

the men's religion helped them to acquire the discipline required of a soldier.

By mutual understanding British officers never entered the temple or took part in religious festivals, except perhaps to attend a V.C.O.s' celebration teaparty. On religious holidays arrangements were made to have the maximum number of men off duty to enjoy themselves, and appropriate greetings were conveyed to the Subedar-Major, Pandit and all ranks. Similarly on Christmas morning the Pandit and the V.C.O.s would come to the officers' mess for drinks, and to convey their greetings. Only once in my service did I become involved with the temple.

In 1946, I was commanding the Dogra Regimental Centre at Jullundur, which was regarded as the home of the regiment. The Dogras wished to have the temple enlarged and improved, adding a separate room for the wives and daughters, who were prevented by *purdah* from sharing a room with the men. A screen was planned to conceal the women, but to enable them to see the idol, altar and priest. I was very interested in the project, especially a niche for the war roll of honour book, and was able to contribute a substantial sum for the cost from regimental funds.

The best builder in the place was a Muslim, and I was surprised when no objection was raised to Muslims doing the reconstruction. The builder was just as enthusiastic as Pandit Hari Krishan, Subedar-Major Sher Singh and myself, and we had endless meetings over designs and plans. The result was a greatly improved and attractive *mandir*.

As a special honour British officers were invited to the opening ceremony, at which the congregation removed their shoes at the door, and sat closely packed on the floor. Apparently the ladies were delighted with their special wing, which was occupied for the first time. The Pandit sat in front of the idol and altar, chanting prayers and performing certain rituals, supported occasionally by the singing of the congregation. Offerings were made by people kneeling before the idol, and placing money on the altar. Then very much to my surprise the Pandit invited me to make an address, a rare honour, as the occasions must have been few when a Christian was permitted to give a sermon in a Hindu temple. After recovering from the shock, I felt it would be appropriate to say a few words about the common purpose of church and temple.

The gist of what I said was, 'The Hindu goes to the *mandir* to worship Parmatma, and to pray for help and guidance in his life, and for the same purpose the Christian goes to church to worship God. Both *mandir* and church are houses of the Almighty, whom we approach in our different and traditional ways. In keeping with deep devotion to your religion, you have enlarged and improved this *mandir* at the home of the regiment. I am particularly pleased that a sacred place has been found for the regimental Roll of Honour. I wish to join in thanking the Pandit, Subedar Major, and all those who have helped by work or offerings to rebuild the *mandir*. As always it will play a noble part in the life of the Dogra Regiment.'

Religion seemed to dominate the lives of people in India, whether they were Hindu, Sikh, Muslim or Buddhist, and, for daring into that world of religious fanatics, the Christian missionaries showed the greatest courage. They preached that the man-to-God and man-to-man relationships were more important than rituals and ceremonies, and expressed their faith by building schools and hospitals to serve their fellow men. In attempting to convert Muslims and high caste Hindus they met often with bitter hostility, and rarely with success, because changing their faith would mean loss of caste, and grave disruptions in their families. The missionaries had more success with the low castes and untouchables, to whom conversion gave dignity and hope. Despite all obstacles the missionaries firmly established the Church in India which has several million Christians today.

During the Raj religion did not prevent Christian, Hindu, Muslim and Sikh from serving amicably in the same regiment. Believing in a spiritual God all had something in common, even if their faiths were expressed differently. Communal strife often broke out in India under the guise of religion, but did not spread to the army, which could be trusted to maintain the peace impartially. Religious tolerance in the army, however, depended largely on British influence, and failed to endure after independence in 1947 when the country was beset by communal strife.

According to his caste, a Dogra Rajput in the army believed that he was born into the world to be a soldier, and to fulfil his life had to be a good soldier, with a clean conduct sheet and held in respect. If on a sweltering hot day a Dogra was lethargic on parade, a V.C.O. or N.C.O. only had to say to him, "Aren't you a Rajput?" Nothing bestirred him more.

Before the British occupation the Dogras were constantly at war, with Muslims, Sikhs or the neighbouring state, and therefore had a long tradition as warriors. Moreover, life in the unproductive hills was hard and difficult, conditions which bred courage, discipline, loyalty to the raja and clan, and all the qualities of a soldier. The hereditary loyalty of the Dogra to his chief and clan was extended to his officer and regiment. To serve with such men was a great pleasure, and, inspired by them, British officers returned in full all the respect and affection they received.

In general appearance high caste Dogras, such as Brahmans and Rajputs, have good well-bred features with light-brown complexions, are lightly built, and in stature men average about 5 feet 5 inches. Although usually lightweights, they, like most hill farmers, are hardy and possess great endurance. As soldiers on the north-west frontier they proved on many occasions that they were particularly suited for mountain warfare.

Dogras are devoted to their homes and native hills, and a man from, say, Kangra, will affectionately refer to his district as "my Kangra". From his small army pay a Dogra made every sacrifice to save and send money home, and when setting off on annual leave was invariably accompanied by a black steel trunk packed with clothes, a garment or two for each member of the family. The joy at the other end can be imagined, when Ram Singh arrived with his black box, for his wife and children had perhaps not seen him for a year.

At home Dogras led a simple peasant life confined mainly to agriculture, herding, building or maintaining their cottages, and taking part in religious ceremonies and festivals. Some recruits arrived illiterate, probably because the nearest school was too far from home; the rest would have been to a primary school, and a fair number to a secondary school. Although Dogras were full of common sense and anxious to learn, the process was slow and painstaking, but skills acquired were used proficiently. With the clear eyesight of countrymen they were excellent shots.

When the First Sikh War ended in 1846, the British occupied the hill country between the rivers Sutlej and Beas, and so first came into contact with the Dogras, which began a century of close and friendly partnership, especially in the army. That same year the first Dogra battalion was raised at Kangra by Captain J. W. V. Stephen, as the 2nd Regiment of Infantry of the Frontier Brigade, and known as the Dogra *Paltan*. After various changes in name this battalion finally became 2nd Bn. 12th Frontier Force Regiment of mixed composition. Dogras were enlisted in several mixed Punjab and Frontier Force Regiments, and eventually in their own all-Dogra Regiment.

The old Indian Army was not composed of short service conscripts but long service regulars, of whom few left before earning a small pension after 12 years' service, and many served longer. The men were volunteers and enjoyed serving, and that accounted for the fine spirit in all regiments.

Dogra Rajputs invariably owned ancestral farmland, although generally small in acreage. Agriculture was the basis of their economy, supplemented by army pay or pension. Families were usually large with several brothers, and while one or two stayed at home to manage the farm, others enlisted. Women and children of soldiers absent from home lived on the family farm, and were cared for by the rest of the joint family. Dogras were rarely worried about being separated from their families, who were perfectly happy and secure in the ancestral home, surrounded by loyal relations. Annually men were given two months' leave in the summer, and a further ten days in emergency to deal with any problem at home, such as a birth or a religious ceremony.

A permanent home and a secure family background were major factors in providing the stability of the Indian Army; between home and regiment men appeared to live happy and contented lives. In peace stations married quarters were provided for a small proportion of the men, but with Dogras a waiting list was rare, for they mostly preferred to leave their families at home. Nearly all the men in a battalion were married. Soldiers were very eligible in the marriage market, and most of them married soon after joining, the grooms being about 17 years of age and the brides a few years younger.

The tendency was for a family, or several families of a hamlet, to adopt a certain regiment, and son would follow father into "our *paltan*". Many pensioned Dogras have brought their sons to me, and the introduction has been something like this, "This is my son Tej Singh, who has come to enlist in our *paltan* to take my place. He is a smart lad and has been educated up to the 6th class. Treat him as your own son, train him well, and don't forget to promote him." It was rather like a father entering his son at his old school, and introducing him to the headmaster; there was no better relationship. At the periodic regimental re-union of pensioners, Tej Singh's father would tramp for two days, and spend a day in the train, to see his son on parade and at sport, and to refresh happy memories of his own service days.

By 1938 I had served with Dogras for 19 years, but my knowledge of their country was confined to a few motor roads, and I had failed to get off the beaten track and live among them. In a good natured way I was often reproached by the men for not having made myself more acquainted with their homeland. The opportunity came when I was appointed to command the Territorial Battalion.

On 1 May 1938, I relieved Major M. L. Hayne (later Brigadier) at Jullundur. The territorial soldiers had dispersed to their homes at the end of winter training, and only a few members of the permanent staff were present. A solitary clerk, Havildar Rikhi Ram, occupied the office, and two storemen looked after the armoury, clothing and equipment stores. The camp site would remain deserted until winter, when the civilian soldiers again assembled for training. During the summer, I would have spells of leave totalling two months in the hill resort of Dalhousie with Elsa, spend occasional days in Jullundur preparing for winter training, and devote most of my time to recruiting. Touring for recruits would take me not only to the Dogra villages, but as far as Lahoul in the higher Himalayas, for, unlike the regular battalions, we had a company of Lahoulis.

Before the Second World War began on 3 September, I had completed two summer recruiting seasons and one winter training season. The battalion recruiting area was mainly in the foothills of the eastern region, but we also tried to interest men from the higher mountains in Chamba and Kulu. They were not orthodox Rajputs, had no military tradition, and, with very rare exceptions, showed no desire to serve. Also, accustomed to the cool air of the mountains they dreaded the heat of the plains in summer. However, that was not the character of all the highlanders in the Himalayas, for further east the Gurkhas, living at high altitudes, were ardent soldiers, and so were our Lahoulis, who lived even higher.

The expression, martial classes, was common in India, as only men of certain castes and regions were considered to make good soldiers, which in the area I covered was well illustrated by Chamba State and Kangra District. The Rajput element was strong in Kangra, and every village had a number of serving and pensioned soldiers. Before the Raj, the area had been constantly at war, defending itself and participating in the power struggle for the Punjab, which naturally bred warriors. Chamba, screened by high mountains, had remained remote from the conflicts in the Punjab, and its people had developed into peaceful castes of small cultivators and shepherds, who had no desire to be soldiers or to move away from home.

In preparing a tour programme there were three main considerations: the time of year, which governed temperatures; the monsoon, at its height from mid-July to mid-September; the need to deal with the office work every few weeks. I decided to deal with the hot lower altitudes in the spring and autumn, and to ascend to the cool higher slopes when the plains began to bake. During the monsoon the mule tracks were difficult, as unbridged hill streams, normally fordable, became deep torrents. So in the rains I was confined mainly to the few motor roads, the office in Jullundur and leave in Dalhousie.

The country was dotted with small resthouses for administrative officers on tour, which had a few crudely furnished rooms, providing the minimum comfort. Elementary cooking was done by bearer Feroz Din on an open wood fire, and I was frequently informed that cooking was not his job; the results certainly proved it. Off the motor road the resthouses were about 12 or 15 miles apart, a day's march. Some tours I was able to do by car, but most meant walking or riding along rough tracks and hiring a pack mule and sometimes a riding pony. I preferred the slow pace of the rough tracks. The mule carried my suitcase, and the bedding rolls of Feroz Din, the mule owner and myself.

Men of the battalion were informed of my visit, and many came to see me at the resthouses, sometimes with recruits, whom I enlisted on the spot. Apart from recruiting, I was able to keep in touch with the men, and assist them in their problems with government officials, either by drafting letters or by personal intervention.

The leisurely pace of the tours helped me to become acquainted with the country and the people. At the base of the hills the region is somewhat arid, dusty and hot in summer, but on climbing higher the temperature drops, pine trees appear and the scenery improves. Towards the north the hills and mountains rise majestically in tiers towards the snow-capped peaks of the Himalayas, and I was able to appreciate why the Dogras regarded their homeland with such pride and affection.

On the plains the villages were compact and congested, relics of the days when they were built for security and defence. The highest houses in the centre provided all-round observation, while on the perimeter lower buildings and boundary walls could easily be converted into breastworks. No land was wasted and crops were grown right up to the outer walls. Without organised sanitation refuse was left rotting in the narrow lanes, and the outskirts of a village were used as open latrines. The only scavengers were the birds and pi-dogs, and to the unaccustomed the flies and smell were nauseating.

In the hills, urban areas also suffered from undisposed refuse, but sanitation in rural areas was helped by greater dispersion in small hamlets and farmsteads. This was due to the conformation of the hilly country, the desire of farmers to live on their land, and the wish of small communities to have privacy and seclusion. Clusters of cottages were often located amid pleasant and picturesque surroundings. The houses, mostly two-storeyed, were built of sun-dried bricks, with roofs of thatch or slate, and outside walls plastered with red or light-coloured earth. In front of the house was a clean open space for sitting out, with the whole encircled by trees and bushes for privacy.

Brahmans and Rajputs always occupied the highest and most secluded sites, for it was not tolerated for a man of low caste to erect his dwelling on high ground overlooking the homes of those of higher birth. In congested areas the low castes generally lived on the outer fringes. Visited at all hours of the day by people wishing to pray or make offerings, a temple was generally situated on an attractive hillock, and in the evening resounded with enthusiastic singing and the clanging of cymbals.

Agricultural land in the hills was rarely as productive as irrigated land on the plains, and with the shortage of food even uneconomic stony patches were cultivated. Fields, often small and terraced on steep slopes, were ploughed with difficulty by teams of two bullocks. Land not cultivated was grazed by cattle, sheep and goats. Good harvests depended on seasonal rain, and especially on the monsoon, which sometimes failed, causing hunger and hardship.

On a few occasions I stayed with Dogra officers, all big landowners with the status of squires, and possessing substantial homes. My hosts had impeccable manners and treated me with old-fashioned courtesy. Interesting talks with them, away from the formality of the regiment, greatly increased my knowledge of Dogras.

With strict *purdah* a male guest, not related to the family, had to be isolated from the women, and therefore could be accommodated only by the owner of a large house. I found close contact with *purdah* somewhat embarrassing, and was almost afraid to leave my room in case I should disturb any of the ladies, for even white-haired grannies scurried for cover when I emerged, refusing to risk allegations of immodesty by permitting their faces to be seen by a stranger.

As the family was forbidden by caste to eat with me, food was brought to my room. Meals were served on a brass tray, and usually consisted of two different kinds of curry eaten with rice or wheat *chapattis*, followed by a sweet or two and fresh fruit. I was given a knife, fork and spoon, though Indians ate with their hands, which were formally washed before and after meals. With only two meals a day, it seemed a long wait from a late breakfast until dinner in the evening.

One of my hosts provided a home for an elderly *sadhu* (holy man) who had left his own home to devote his life to prayer and meditation. Even on small matters decisions were not made without the advice of the *sadhu*, who therefore exercised much influence on the life of the family. Each day he sallied forth with his begging bowl and wandered around the hamlets, bringing back village news and gossip, to be enjoyed especially by the secluded women.

By residing in their villages it was possible to see how Dogras lived, some well-off but most of them poor, with small cramped houses in which the crude furniture consisted of little more than beds. The few rooms were carefully cleaned, but with overcrowding and poor storage facilities difficult to keep tidy. A housewife took pride in her kitchen, with brass pots and pans gleaming, though she must have found cooking an ordeal, squatting in front of an open wood and cow dung fire, enveloped in smoke.

When the Territorials assembled for training in Jullundur, I endeavoured to return the hospitality I received on tour by inviting Dogra I.C.O.s to meals at my home. Whereas in their villages they would not risk to be seen eating with a person of a different religion or of lower caste, in the regiment it was impossible to keep up this prohibition, at least for officers. While Hindu other ranks were able to feed separately, officers of all religions and castes had to live and feed in the same mess. However, when catering for or entertaining Hindu officers care had to be taken not to serve beef, which would constitute a grave insult and blunder.

On one of my tramps through Kangra District I arrived at a big village called Sujanpur Tira near the River Beas, to find a large crowd had gathered on the village green for an address by the Master of the Radha Swamis, a new religious sect. When I arrived at the resthouse, a tall Sikh with a drawn *kirpan* stood guard over the gate and barred my way. He said the Master was in residence and there was no room, to which I replied that I had reserved a room with every intention of occupying it. Eventually I did so.

That evening I received an invitation to meet the Master, Baba Sawan Singh Ji Maharaj, and was greeted by a handsome, white-bearded old Sikh, of great personal charm. He said that he aimed to unite people in a common religion, superimposed on but not interfering with their present religion, and so put an end to strife and bloodshed. There were three simple rules of membership.

(a) A clean and upright life.
(b) No eating of meat, fish or eggs.
(c) Abstention from intoxicants.

We had a long discussion in which I supported the idea of unity, but disagreed that it could be based on what to eat and drink. I quoted Christ's ruling given in *St. Mark* 7:15, that a man is not defiled by what goes into him, but by what comes out of him; his words and actions. However, I much enjoyed an interesting and friendly talk.

Master Sawan Singh had many followers, and built a fine temple and study centre just north of the Beas bridge between Jullundur and Amritsar. He died in April 1948, soon after the terrible communal massacres in the Punjab, with heavy losses in the country surrounding his temple. He must have been deeply grieved in failing to prevent the disaster which he feared.

My most memorable trip was to the friendly Lahoulis, a small mountain tribe numbering only about ten thousand. Lahoul, above 10,000 feet, includes the two valleys of the small rivers Chandra and Bhaga, which unite at the village of Tanda, to form the great River Chenab. The motor road ends at Manali, at 6,200 feet, at the head of the Kulu valley. Thence to the high Chandra valley is two days march over the Rohtang Pass, following a narrow pony track, which zigzags up a sheer mountain side to 13,400 feet. Just below the pass the track passes the source of the River Beas, a favourite place of pilgrimage for Dogras. On reaching the crest of the Rohtang there is a breath-taking view of the valley flanked by giant mountains, and of the first Lahouli village, Khoksar.

The Rohtang divides two worlds, the one Hindu and the other Buddhist, with striking contrasts in the features and dress of the people, as also in their environment and climate. With rich cultivation and pine clad slopes, the Kulu valley is luxuriantly green, and enjoys a pleasant climate without severe extremes of heat or cold. The people are essentially Indian and Hindu temples dominate the scattered villages. On the Lahoul side of the high ridge the mountains are bare with few trees, white above the snow line, grey and brown below. The villages are small and compact, lying at the bottom of deep narrow valleys, whose sides rise in walls of rock to 18,000 feet. Almost every village is over-looked by a Buddhist monastery, built on a narrow ledge high up on the mountain.

In appearance the Lahoulis are more Tibetan than Indian. The young are good looking, strongly built and healthy, and invariably greeted one with an infectious grin. The harsh winters and bitter winds age people prematurely, and the old develop leathery, deeply wrinkled faces, but the friendly grin remains. Summer is devoted to urgent collection of food and fuel, before villages become snow-bound and isolated in winter. When the Lahoulis are cooped up in their houses by cold and snow, the main industry is spinning and weaving of rough woollen cloth. Cold and boredom in winter result in the men drinking excessively the home brewed and distilled alcohols, *chhang* (beer) and *arak* (spirit).

The Lahoulis do not suffer from caste prejudices, nor observe *purdah*, and it was a change to see women without veils, moving about freely and cheerfully. They appeared to do as much heavy work as the men, especially in gathering winter fuel from the mountains, which, due to the natural scarcity of trees, entailed arduous walks and climbs.

My destination was Kyelang, two marches from Khoksar, and near the home of two Lahouli officers of the Territorial Battalion, Captain Thakur Pratap Chand and his brother Lieutenant (later Colonel) Thakur Prithi Chand. There they very kindly arranged for me to visit a monastery, and to see a religious dance by lamas. On arrival at the gate we were greeted by a fanfare sounded on long brass horns, and accompanied by drums and cymbals. Similar music was provided for the dance, which began with the appearance of demons and evil spirits, who had come to torment the world. Wearing brilliant silk robes and huge grotesque masks, they whirled and gyrated in a circle. Next the good spirits appeared, similarly disguised to deceive the demons, with whom they mingled in the dance. Suddenly the good spirits revealed themselves, and proceeded to destroy the demons in a battle, symbolised by sticks clashing in rhythm with the drums and cymbals.

After the dance we were entertained at a tea and drink party, at which all sat on the floor in a large room with backs to the wall. The tea with rancid butter floating on top was an acquired taste, but the *arak*, sweet and fiery, was quite palatable. Pratap warned me that it had a powerful delayed action, and that the jovial lamas would be delighted to see me carried out. It certainly was potent, but I managed to make a dignified exit on my feet, with the band playing another fanfare at the gate.

In Kyelang, where he worked, I met Mr. Friedal A. Peter, a Moravian missionary, who said he had tried in vain to introduce skis, which he himself used a great deal in winter. He considered their use would make life less restricted for the Lahoulis, when for months they were snow-bound in their villages, but he failed to overcome their superstition. On the surrounding slopes there was a great danger of avalanches, which the Lahoulis connected with evil spirits, who they feared, if disturbed by skiers, would bring down the deadly slides of snow and rock.

On the return journey, at Khoksar I was asked by a Dogra *gaddi* (goatherd) to shoot a red bear which was killing his goats. Hardy *gaddis* from Kangra and Mandi brought their flocks up to Lahoul in search of summer grazing, climbing higher and deeper into the mountains as the snow receded. Usually they had large savage dogs to keep off predators, but the dog of the man who approached me had recently died. Deciding to spend a night there, I accompanied the goatherd to his camp, just below the snow at about 14,000 feet. The camp was merely an open site on a ledge, with water from a spring, and a stone shelter for the *gaddi*, just large enough to cover his bed.

Due to the ground being well fertilised by the sheep, a rich crop of weeds had grown with thick roots like carrots, which were the main object of the bear's nightly visits, though it occasionally varied its diet with a goat. There was ample evidence of its digging the previous night, and the *gaddi* expected it to return after dark. I decided to sit up with a torch attached to my rifle, and the *gaddi* offered to keep watch near by. I was accompanied by Freckles, a young Dalmatian bitch, who had replaced Brownie when she died, but knowing she would not keep quiet in the ambush, I sent her back to the resthouse with the porter who had carried up my valise. To my dismay she escaped and returned after dark.

Keeping awake with difficulty, after a few hours I heard a disturbance among the goats, and Freckles growled. Grabbing the rifle, I jumped up and flashed the torch, but saw no bear. The *gaddi* had left his post and I found him asleep in his den, with boulders blocking the entrance; apparently he had decided that discretion was the better part of valour. Following his example I decided to lose no more sleep, and was not disturbed again.

Next morning we searched the mountain until exhausted by the rarefied air, without being rewarded by even a glimpse of the bear. However, experiencing the life of a wandering Dogra *gaddi* had made the venture worthwhile.

Cultivation was restricted in the narrow valleys of Lahoul and failed to produce enough food, much of which had to be imported. To pay for this the main export was Himalayan *kuth* (Latin name *Saussurea lappa*), a perennial plant of which the root is used in making incense. Minor exports were homespun woollen cloth and blankets.

The seeds of the *kuth* plant had been recently introduced by the enterprise of Friedal Peter from Kashmir, where hitherto the plant, grown in high valleys similar to those of Lahoul, had been a strictly-guarded government monopoly. As *kuth* would grow only in special, rare conditions it had a very high market value, especially in China. Flourishing crops in Lahoul soon increased the prosperity of a poor area.

Apart from exporting their own produce, the Lahoulis were active carriers and traders, forming a link in the commerce between Tibet and India. To India they brought commodities such as wool and *pashmina*—expensive silken wool from the under fur of the Tibetan goat. In exchange they returned with food and manufactured goods, and tea grown in the Kangra Valley. In summer, with their pack ponies traders undertook long and arduous journeys over high mountain passes.

It was interesting to compare these frontiersmen with the *trans-frontier* Pathans, both living in arid and unproductive mountain regions. The latter were lawless, murderous to their neighbours, and inveterate brigands. In contrast the Lahoulis, with their Buddhist culture, were law-abiding, peaceful and good neighbours, who subsisted by honest endeavour and hard work in most difficult conditions. Though peaceful they did not lack moral courage and made fine soldiers.

Touring in their country increased my knowledge of the Dogras and Lahoulis and confirmed my high regard for them. Even when not personally known, the friendly reception I received in villages, because I was a British officer, was typical of their loyalty to the Raj. They were among our best friends in India.

CHAPTER V

THE SECOND WORLD WAR

In the prewar Indian Army there were 19 Indian and 10 Gurkha infantry regiments, 18 active cavalry regiments, and other arms and services. As the size of regiments varied, the proportionate strength is clearer from the number of battalions; Indian 78, Gurkha 20, cavalry equivalent to 18. The total strength amounted to about 180,000, commanded by 3,000 British and 500 Indian officers. By the end of the war these numbers had increased to a total of over two million, with 34,500 British and 8,300 Indian officers.

Before the war the rôle of the Indian Army was internal security, protection of the north-west border districts from raids by *trans*-border tribes, and defence against adjoining countries, none of which had a modern army. An attack by a major power was the responsibility of Great Britain. In view of its limited rôle, and financial stringency, the army was not mechanised or fully equipped with modern weapons, having only horse cavalry and artillery, and infantry with mule transport. There were no armoured units or anti-tank weapons, and only a few anti-aircraft guns.

The officers and men of that small army, though largely deprived of modern weapons, were tough and superbly trained under active service conditions on the north-west frontier, and provided a perfect nucleus for expansion and modernisation in war. Increasing to over ten times its peace-time strength, the Indian Army together with the British Army provided six mixed divisions in the Middle East and Italy, two in Malaya, and ten in Burma; in those divisions most of the infantry battalions were Indian, but nearly all the artillery regiments were British. Moreover the north-west frontier was protected, and internal security maintained in India.

While the British Commonwealth stood alone against Germany and Italy, the Indian divisions in the Middle East were vital for the defence of that area. Later when Japan entered the war, the Indian Army played a major part in her defeat. The great expansion and contribution of that army, composed entirely of volunteers, was made possible only by the deep bond that existed between British officers and the martial classes. It was remarkable how that withstood the national and anti-war propaganda of the Congress politicians. The soldiers stood firm in their belief that the safety and future of India could only be assured in co-operation with the officers they trusted. Three thousand regular British officers contributed to victory out of all proportion to their number, by raising and commanding an army of over two millions.

It is proposed to give a short account of the 17th Dogra Regiment in the Second World War, during which it had to resolve problems and difficulties, typical of those confronting the Indian Army as a whole. This account does not cover all the Dogras who fought in the war, for they were also enlisted in five mixed infantry regiments and five mixed cavalry regiments. Only the Dogra Regiment was composed entirely of Dogras. By chance no Dogra battalions fought in western theatres, and all six battalions which took the field did so against the Japanese in Malaya and Burma.

The regiment began the war with a regimental training centre for recruits, three active battalions (front line), and one territorial battalion (internal security). During the war six more battalions were raised, making a total of ten. In one chapter it is not possible to condense the war record of ten battalions, but to tell only a small part of their story. Accounts are given very briefly of some battalions with which I did not serve, and in more detail of two with which I did serve. Many of the events mentioned were trivial, but help to portray an Indian Regiment playing its part in the war.

Of the three prewar regular Dogra battalions only the 1st survived to fight in the final victory. Its first action was against the Japanese in Arakan in December 1942, and except for a

H

period of rest the following summer, it remained in that theatre until March 1944. As the Japanese hammered at the gates of India fighting was bitter and costly, in arduous conditions of heat, damp and malaria, with the battalion losing many fine men, including its first C.O. in the war, Lt.-Colonel R. A. Cropper. Dick was immensely popular, and the battalion history records that 'the whole battalion wept' at his death.

The main Japanese offensive to invade India was launched on the Assam front, to which the 5th Indian Division, including the 1st Battalion, was moved by air from Arakan to reinforce the hard-pressed defenders of Kohima and Imphal. The action at Nunshigam, on 13 April 1944, was typical of the fierce battles which turned the tide against the Japanese.

After heavy fighting the Japanese had seized the hill of Nunshigam, 7 miles from Imphal, headquarters of 4th Corps. The threat to Imphal and its airfield was so serious that the hill had to be recaptured at all costs, a task entrusted to the 1/17th Dogras under Lt.-Colonel E. G. Woods, supported by the tanks of 'B' Squadron 3rd Carabiniers. The attack was led by two companies and the tanks. The company commanders Majors L. A. Jones and H. W. Alden were severely wounded, and all the officers of the Carabiniers killed. Despite heavy losses the attack continued under Subedar Ranbir Singh, Subedar Tiru Ram and Squadron Sergeant-Major Craddock until all the defenders were killed and the hill secured. At last the Japanese were to taste the bitterness of defeat.

After the battle of Imphal the 1st Battalion took part in the pursuit of the Japanese to the River Chindwin, and later in the advance from Meiktila to Rangoon, fighting in many desperate encounters. In recognition of the battalion's outstanding record in the 14th Army, it provided the Indian guard of honour at the surrender ceremony in Rangoon. Tragically that did not mean the end of the war, for during five months' fighting in Java the battalion lost many of the heroes of the Burma campaign.

The 2/17 Dogras, my parent battalion, went to Malaya in April 1939 as part of the normal peace-time garrison, and, before the Japanese invasion, had well over two years' experience of training in Malayan conditions. Being overseas it had not suffered as much as the 1st and 3rd in losing experienced men to form new battalions, and had as many as eight regular officers, headed by Lt.-Colonel S. C. Scott, D.S.O., M.C.

Most of the battalions hurriedly sent to Malaya were composed mainly of recruits, and recently commissioned officers with no experience of Indian troops or jungle war. Therefore it was ironical that a strong battalion like the 2nd was not in action before the surrender, except for its carrier platoon. When its position near Kota Tinggi had been outflanked by the Japanese advancing further west, the battalion was sent to defend the island of Palau Tekong, which guarded the Johore Straits and the Naval Base. The island was never attacked, and when ordered to surrender, all had to endure the agony of captivity without the satisfaction of having fought.

The 3/17th Dogras arrived in Singapore on 11 November 1940, and later fired the first shot in the war against Japan. As part of the 8th Infantry Brigade, the battalion commanded by Lt.-Colonel G. A. Preston, was given the task to hold 14 miles of beach north-east of Kota Bharu. On such a wide front it could only man small posts half a mile apart, thus providing no more than a thin screen. The defence of the beaches required adequate reserves for counter attack, which were not available.

Under cover of darkness in the early hours of 8 December 1941, Japanese landing craft headed for a creek in the middle of the Dogra position, and despite heavy losses gained a footing. The few posts covering the creek fought to the last man. All efforts to dislodge the Japanese failed, and they continued to pour in troops and penetrate inland. By nightfall the Dogras were still holding the beaches either side of the creek, but during the night were ordered to withdraw to a position just north of Kota Bharu. So for them began the disheartening retreat to Singapore. On a beach held by the 3rd Dogras the Japanese erected a memorial to 3,000 of their dead, to commemorate their hardest battle in Malaya.

In the retreat down the Malay Peninsula the battalion was

constantly in action, and its strength gradually whittled away. From about 800 only 6 officers and 107 other ranks remained to cross the causeway on to Singapore Island, where two more British officers were lost in the final battle. It was a sad end for the gallant 3rd Battalion, whose battle honours in the First World War included Neuve Chapelle and the Tigris.

The following extract is from a letter from Major-General B. W. Key. 'Your 3rd Battalion was under my command at Kota Bharu at the time the landing took place, and was actually holding the beach where the landing took place. Although one company was on a front of 8,000 yards, and another on a front of 10,000 yards, they put up a magnificent show, and were to a great extent responsible for the casualties inflicted on the Japs. According to Japanese prisoners captured at the time, the Japs had to form two Regiments (Brigades) into one as a result of their losses. The 3rd Battalion may very well be proud of the fight they put up at Kota Bharu.'

After the German victory in France and the withdrawal from Dunkirk, the British Commonwealth stood alone, and expansion of the Indian Army became urgent. The first new active Dogra battalion was raised at Peshawar, on 1 October 1940, by Lt.-Colonel E. R. M. Hall, made up by cadres from the regular battalions and recruits from the Centre. In a year the 4th Battalion was ready for a frontier rôle and posted to Razmak in Waziristan, an ideal training ground, where it remained for two years. Many new units suffered from taking the field without adequate training, but when the 4th moved to the Burma front in March 1944 it was ready for the fray.

The battalion, then commanded by Lt.-Colonel R. P. Taylor, joined the 20th Indian Division at Imphal. After crossing the rivers Chindwin and Irrawaddy the division reached Wundwin to cut off the Japanese in Mandalay from the south. In the last stage of that most successful outflanking move Rupert Taylor was killed while leading his men near Pya, a great loss to the battalion. He was succeeded by Lt.-Colonel E. B. Colson. In the final drive for Rangoon the 20th Division attacked down the left bank of the Irrawaddy to beyond Prome, and during the advance the 4/17th was constantly in action against the retreating enemy. On the surrender of the Japanese the battalion formed part of the occupation forces, first in French Indo-China and then in Celebes.

In the First World War Edward Colson's father had been killed in action with the 41st Dogras in Mesopotamia, but the Second War ended more happily for Edward. Soon after the battalion arrived in Saigon he met his future wife, Nursing Sister Mary Gavin, Queen Alexandra's Imperial Military Nursing Service, who had served with the 14th Army, much of the time with a Forward Casualty Clearing Station; a brave Dogra bride.

The 5th Battalion was raised at Jullundur on 1 February 1941 by Lt.-Colonel H. R. Power. A nucleus of trained personnel was provided by other Dogra battalions, but most of the men were recruits. There were a few regular British officers, but the majority had emergency commissions, with little training or experience and only a slight knowledge of Urdu. On completion of initial training the battalion joined the 17th Indian Division, which was being trained and equipped for the Middle East.

When the Japanese threat developed in the Far East the 5/17th, as part of the 46th Infantry Brigade, suddenly moved to South Burma with the 17th Division. The battalion was only half trained and that for mechanised desert war, very different from jungle warfare to which it was committed. It reached the battle area on 1 February 1942, its first birthday, and relieved the 2nd Bn. King's Own Yorkshire Light Infantry in a position covering the road and rail bridges across the River Bilin.

Tied to the coastal road by its motor transport, the 17th Division held as far south as Moulmein. The Japanese, trained and equipped for the jungle, were able to move across country, and made constant attempts to outflank and cut off the British. Too late, a decision was made to withdraw to a more secure position behind the River Sittang. Before the two rear brigades, the 16th and 46th, could reach the only bridge, the Japanese by a wide flanking move arrived first and attacked the bridgehead troops. To prevent them falling into the hands of the Japanese, and so open the road to Rangoon, the bridge and all boats were destroyed, marooning the two brigades on the east bank. Cut off from supplies they could not resist for long.

For the men of the 5th Dogras there was no escape but to swim the fast flowing river, 1,000 yards across. Such a feat was beyond the endurance of most, and of those who attempted to cross only 4 British officers and about 150 men reached the far bank. Henry Power, Subedar-Major Relu and the rest were taken prisoner on 24 February 1942, nine days after the fall of Singapore. The remnants of the battalion fought their way out of Burma with the 17th Division. Relu escaped from a working party in North Burma, a rare achievement, and after walking through the jungle for five days reached some Chinese outposts. Back in the regiment he received a hero's welcome.

Within a few days three battalions of Dogras had been lost in Singapore and Burma, a heavy blow felt not only in the regiment but throughout the Dogra country. The Dogras accepted the reverse with courage, and the usual comment was, 'It is *kismet* (fate) but we shall win in the end'.

With the disasters in Malaya and Burma the need for more front-line units became urgent. In addition to providing them the Indian Army had to protect the north-west frontier (70,000 troops), and to maintain internal security (130,000 troops). To some extent the problem was solved by moving trained units from the frontier to the war, new units from internal security to the frontier, and by raising more new units for internal security.

Of the Dogra Battalions that fought in the war five have been mentioned, and an account of the Machine Gun Battalion will be given later. Two more battalions, the 6th (Territorial) and 7th (newly raised), were moved to the frontier to release more highly trained units for the war. To avoid repetition an account will be given only of the 6th, as the experience of the 7th in defending the frontier was very similar. Finally the 25th and 26th Garrison Battalions were raised for internal security and none proved more reliable.

The new battalions were composed mostly of young recruits with a nucleus of regulars. All had the splendid spirit that is part of a volunteer army, and trained with enthusiasm and determination to reach operational standard. The main problem was to find enough volunteers to fill the ranks.

At first recruiting for fighting units was restricted to the martial classes, but when the supply ran out other selected classes were accepted. Thus the strength of the Dogra Regiment was completed by taking Dogras slightly below Rajput in caste and Brahman farmers from the United Provinces. The experiment to recruit men older than early twenty failed, as they took too long to train and toughen, but the intake was greatly increased by lowering the peace-time standards of height and weight. It was found that smaller and lighter men, although somewhat handicapped in carrying heavy equipment, otherwise made good soldiers. Generally the response was magnificent, especially from our old and staunch friends the martial classes, and adequate numbers were obtained by opening the gates wider.

The Regimental Centre at Jullundur was the hub of the regiment. Its main tasks were : to train recruits whose numbers gradually increased from a few hundred in peace to as many thousand in war; to provide a convalescent home for men recovering from wounds or from illness contracted on field service; to maintain records of every man in the regiment and to send a monthly allowance to his family.

The two battalions to be described now are those with whom I served. Throughout the war years I was a battalion commander, and therefore in close touch with Dogra soldiers. The greater part of that period I did not spend in a fighting area, but in training, internal security and frontier defence. Even in those less spectacular rôles, during critical years, the loyalty of our Indian troops was a vital factor towards victory.

On the evening of 3 September 1939, I returned to Jullundur from a recruiting tour, feeling hot and thirsty. Off the beaten track, I had not seen a newspaper for some days, and so walked over to the Dogra Centre mess for a drink and to hear the radio news. As the situation in Europe was critical, Lt.-Colonel R. G. Sanders, commanding the Centre, and a few others were there anxiously waiting for the news broadcast, which confirmed our fears by the announcement that war had been declared on Germany.

With the First World War fresh in our minds, it was hard to believe that the people of Western Europe should again set about exterminating each other. Recovering from the shock Reg Sanders and I briefly discussed problems affecting mobilisation, and I left for the barracks to find Rikhi Ram, head clerk of the 11/17th Dogras (Indian Territorial Force) whom I commanded. The clerk, myself and a few storemen were the only members of the battalion present, as the part-time soldiers were all at home, and not due to assemble for annual training until November.

Rikhi was a frail little Dogra, not strong enough for service with an active battalion, but very conscientious and efficient. He took the news very calmly. As mobilisation orders were expected, we quickly checked over our mobilisation scheme, including bundles of envelopes addressed to each man, containing a calling-up notice and a railway warrant. I imagined the concern the notice would cause in many humble peasant homes; taking away Ram Singh the mainstay of his small farm.

During the monsoon, September in Jullundur was intensely hot and humid, and not conducive to the feverish activity of mobilisation. Briefly it involved gathering together territorial officers and men, one British officer, one V.C.O. and a few N.C.O.s from each of the three regular battalions, and most of our stores and equipment from various arsenals. Everything was prearranged in our mobilisation scheme and went smoothly. Men from nearby Hoshiarpur District were the first to arrive, and the last were from distant Lahoul, who took several days to reach railhead. A few did not report through illness, but there was not a single desertion, which was an encouraging start. Indian territorial battalions had not been raised until 1922, and this was the first time that they had been mobilised for war.

When the 11th Battalion mobilised it numbered three regular British officers, some regular V.C.O. and N.C.O. instructors, and about 600 territorials with only sufficient training to provide static guards. Because of age and medical category some of the territorial officers and men proved unfit for arduous service. Initially our main problems were to replace unfit personnel, and to train and harden the others, which meant remaining in Jullundur during the winter, where I was ably assisted by Lieutenants E. C. Gleeson and J. G. D. Lowe.

The territorial I.C.O.s were men of high status in the Dogra country, and so respected by the men. Those who stayed provided a strong element in the unit, but about a third left either for domestic reasons or because they were of low medical category. The two senior Dogras to remain were Captain Thakur Dina Nath and Raja Naurang Singh, and the senior Lahouli was Lieutenant Thakur Prithi Chand. During my two summer tours I had visited the homes of some of the I.C.O.s, which helped me to establish a friendly relationship.

Subedar-Major Shamsher Chand, a burly hearty man, headed the territorial V.C.O.s, who in type and character were similar to their regular counterparts, and, although lacking in military experience, were enthusiastic and anxious to learn. I had visited the villages of many of them, including that of Shamsher, where I met his father Risaldar Suram Chand, a proud old cavalryman. Both had served in the First World War in Hodson's Horse, father as a troop commander and son as a trooper. Suram Chand's favourite anecdote was of a cavalry charge in which he had ridden down a Turk, but had been lame from a wound ever since. Because of his father's disability Shamsher had had to leave the regular army to manage the family estate, but had continued to serve as a territorial. By knowing something of their home background it helped me to gain the confidence of the V.C.O.s.

The first winter of the war was a period of uncertainty, and although the 4th Indian Division had left for the Middle East, Indian troops had not yet been in action. Until the spring of 1940, when Germany invaded France, it was not clear how the war would develop, and whether the Indian Army would be involved to any extent. In the regiment no orders had been received for expansion except for the mobilisation and training of the territorial battalion.

During the summer of 1939 Elsa had become ill, and doctors had advised her to go to England for a change of climate, and therefore when ordered to mobilise I gave up the bungalow and packed our belongings, which remained in store until 1946. However, Elsa made a good recovery, and in November risked the submarine blockade to return to Jullundur, but we decided that the future was too uncertain to furnish another bungalow, and stayed at Chamier's Hotel.

When we began strenuous training it soon became apparent that many of the men were too old and physically weak to make the grade; in peace time the standard of the territorials was far below that of the regular army. Having the Regimental Centre next door was very convenient, and Reg Sanders was most helpful in replacing unfit men, who were only too happy to return home. Long marches under load, day and night exercises, and periods in camp, became the pattern of life. Although only a territorial battalion armed with rifles, we strove to increase our status and become equipped with modern weapons.

The culmination of winter training was a fortnight in camp and an exercise set by the Brigade Commander, R. Dening, and his Brigade Major, A. W. W. Holworthy. When I met Arthur Holworthy in Italy in 1944 he was commanding the famous 4th Indian Division. During the exercise our rôle was withdrawal, and of the Kapurthala State Infantry pursuit and ambush.

Neither side possessed a single motor vehicle, let alone an armoured vehicle, and my mounted reconnaissance troops consisted of a few *sowars* (troopers) on camels. Admittedly we were only internal security troops, but at that time not even front-line units were mechanised. The Indian Army had a long way to go before it could match the German Panzers, which it did in the end, but not before inferior weapons had cost many lives. The ambush was fortunately spotted just in time by the camel scouts, and my military reputation saved.

The battalion now hoped to be promoted on to a higher military plane, but alas our first task was a humble one, to guard the railway, for with the Indian National Congress, the strongest political party, determined to hinder the war effort, sabotage was feared. In June we relieved the 3/14th Punjab Regiment, with headquarters at Lahore, and the battalion scattered over a wide area protecting railway bridges.

The summer of 1940 was full of dramatic events; defeat in Norway and France, retreat from Dunkirk, the exit of France from the war, the entry of Italy, and the Battle of Britain. Our setbacks provided excellent propaganda for subversive movements in India, and also tested and proved the loyalty of the army. A long war seemed inevitable with an ever increasing demand for Indian troops, requiring considerable expansion of the army. A second formation left for the Middle East, the 5th Indian Division. For the 11/17th, dispersed in small posts along the railway, the two enemies were intense heat and monotony, but as usual the Dogras did not complain.

Major Sant Singh joined the battalion as second-in-command, and was the first regular I.C.O. with whom I served. He came from a military family of Jat Sikhs who farmed near Ludhiana, was an outstanding officer and a pleasant companion. Some years ago we enjoyed a visit from him, when he had risen to the rank of Lt.-General in the new Indian Army.

With intense relief we left the railway in the autumn and moved to Peshawar, where the battalion relieved active battalions of static protection duties. There the winter was cold and bracing, and we all recovered from the debilitating effects of summer. It was a pleasant surprise when the 4th Dogras, a new battalion, moved into adjacent barracks, and friendly rivalry soon developed between the two sister battalions.

In the spring of 1941, our turn came for higher training, and we joined a training division at Icharian on the pine covered hills north of Abbottabad. At 4,000 feet, and above the heat of the plains, we faced a much healthier summer than the previous one. The prospect of being raised to first-line status acted as a spur, and all worked with a will. With no guard or protection duties the battalion was able to concentrate on training, which was helped by a divisional training team, who arranged demonstrations and exercises. Modern weapons were still scarce and we were not fully equipped with light automatic machine guns and mortars, but acquired a few with which men trained in relays.

Families were not allowed in the training camps, and so Elsa moved to an hotel in Murree, about ninety miles away, where, anxious to play her part in the war, she became a secretary in Northern Command Headquarters. I was able to join her for a few weeks' leave. For the rest of the war we saw little of each other, as I was either in a non-family frontier post or overseas.

By the autumn the battalion looked very different from the territorials who had assembled in 1939, and could now operate with efficiency and confidence. On 15 September 1941, we were upgraded from territorial to active status, and renumbered 6th Battalion 17th Dogra Regiment. With the Germans threatening the Caucasus and Persia, our next move was to the northwest frontier to help in the digging of a defensive position across the Kurram Valley near Thal. That period has been described in Chapter II, where for clarity frontier experience has been grouped separately.

In January, after the digging had been completed, the battalion moved to join a brigade in Rawalpindi. A few months later a critical situation developed in the East, when the Japanese occupied Malaya and began to invade Burma. To meet the threat to India, troops were being concentrated in Assam, and much to our delight the battalion was ordered to mobilise for a move there.

Mobilisation was almost complete, when the order was countermanded, for it was decided that only units with motor transport would be sent to Assam. Unfortunately we still had mule transport and no men trained as motor drivers. It was a bitter disappointment, and even more so when the 6th Battalion was ordered back to Thal, a fateful decision, because assignment to frontier defence greatly reduced the chances of going to the war.

However, the false mobilisation did produce two good results, for we received several urgently needed young officers and a complete scale of modern weapons. John Lowe, impatient to get to the war, had gallantly volunteered to join Commandos, and had left us. In 1944, he was unfortunately killed while leading a landing party on Sumatra. Some of the older territorial officers, who could not stand the strain of intensive training, had also left to join garrison battalions.

The vacancies were filled by young British emergency commissioned officers (E.C.O.s), whose experience was confined generally to a year or so in the ranks of a British unit, followed by a course with an Officer Cadet Training Unit. By the end of the war the British E.C.O.s comprised about three-quarters of the officers of the Indian Army, and had played a major part in leading it to victory.

The battalion received a good selection of E.C.O.s who showed great enthusiasm and promise, and were well received by the Dogras. The new arrivals reduced the age level of officers, which was very desirable now that the battalion had been raised to the status of a front-line combatant unit.

Nineteeeen hundred and forty-two was a critical year in India. Until then the war had been remote, but the entry of Japan and the rapid loss of Malaya and Burma had brought the conflict very close. Taking advantage of our failures the Congress Party under Mr. Gandhi and Mr. Nehru launched their so-called non-violent 'Quit India' campaign, resulting in riots, murder, and sabotage of communications in strategic areas.

Emotionally the situation placed Indian troops at home under greater strain than those in the field, but they never wavered. The decisive factor was the trust that existed between British officers and Indian soldiers. The latter believed that the safety of India depended on remaining loyal to their officers and their regiment, and that the future of their country should be settled after the defeat of the common enemy. Despite the loss of three Dogra battalions in Malaya and Burma, no martial class remained more loyal than the Dogras, and I heard no word of criticism or defeatism, but only of determination to win the war.

Of the eight active Dogra battalions only the 6th and 7th failed to reach the war; fate decreed that they should guard the frontier. For another year I remained with the 6th Battalion, first at Thal-in-Kurram and then at Mir Ali in Waziristan, a period already covered in Chapter II. In April 1943, I was appointed to command the Machine Gun Battalion in the Middle East, and felt very sad at leaving the 6th, which I had trained and brought up from the nursery. The men called themselves 'Bristow's Own' and I certainly felt part of them. The officers, Subedar-Major Shamsher Chand and the Dogras gave me a farewell not to be forgotten. I was succeeded by Lt.-Colonel H. G. P. Williams.

M.G. Bn. 17th Dogra Regiment was raised by Lt.-Colonel H. A. Oatts at Jullundur, on 15 October 1941, two months before the Japanese attack on Pearl Harbour, and a year before the second battle of Alamein. The officers consisted of a few regulars, and a few Indian and several British E.C.O.s. The V.C.O.s and N.C.O.s taken from the machine gun companies of the three regular battalions were a particularly fine group of prewar regulars, and the hard core of the battalion. The rest, with few exceptions, were young Dogra Rajput recruits.

On 18 June 1942, only eight months after being raised, the battalion sailed for Persia to join the 6th Indian Division, part of the 10th Army, which was disposed in North-West Persia to stop the Germans should they break through the Caucasus, and threaten the oil fields. The danger receded with the famous Russian victory at Stalingrad in January 1943, and the 10th Army gradually dispersed. All its divisions moved to other theatres except the 6th, which remained with Paiforce (Persia and Iraq Force) to protect the oil fields, and the supply lines from the Persian Gulf to Russia.

The battalion disembarked at Bandar Shahpur, and during the short move to Ahwaz, with the temperature up to 135°F, suffered twenty cases of heatstroke. Of these Captain R. C. Simon died, and the unit unfortunately lost a regular officer of great ability. Luckily the destination of the battalion was the Kermanshah-Hamadan area on the high Persian plateau, where the temperature was much cooler. Until November it remained scattered on security duties, and then concentrated with the division at Qasr-i-Shirin for collective training. Of the ten battalions in the division only the M.G. Dogras was new, and because of the youthful appearance of the men called the *bacha* (baby) battalion.

In October the C.O., Henry Oatts, was invalided to India, and much to his regret left the battalion he had so successfully raised and trained. Lt.-Colonel D. J. Wilson-Haffenden, who took his place, left shortly after joining on being promoted. After commanding the 6/17th for five years, I arrived in Iraq, on 26 April 1943, to begin an equally happy command of the Machine Gunners. I formed a very favourable impression of the battalion, although it was very young and inexperienced, and had several new British officers who needed time to learn Urdu. Among the Dogras I felt completely at home, especially on discovering that a third of the V.C.O.s and N.C.O.s came from the machine gun company, which I had commanded in the 2nd Dogras. They included an old friend, Subedar-Major Shankar Singh, who years previously when I was adjutant, had been my assistant as jemadar adjutant.

When I joined the M.G. Battalion, the 6th Division had recently moved to Kifri, north of Baghdad, and remained there until late in summer, with the heat steadily rising and worse than any I had experienced in India. Tents provided little protection from the sun, and the battalion had many cases of heatstroke, but all survived. British troops, unaccustomed to such heat, suffered most and lost several men. There was intense relief when, in the middle of August, the division moved up to Karind at a higher and cooler altitude on the Persian plateau.

For the first time I was with a mechanised unit. During twenty-four years I had served with infantry who normally walked, but the whole M.G. Battalion was carried in motor transport, with its machine guns in armoured carriers. With much to learn, I was glad to attend a Unit Commanders' Course at Gaza, and later a Mountain Warfare Course in Syria. The course at Gaza increased my knowledge in the handling of motor transport, but far more valuable was the course in Syria, based on recent and new experience in Italy, our probable destination. I returned with clear ideas on future training, realising that we should have to rely less on motor vehicles, and to be prepared to carry our heavy weapons in mountainous country. This would present no problem to the hardy Dogra hillmen, and the Persian hills provided an ideal training ground.

By the spring of 1944 the battalion was in good shape, and there were strong indications that the division would be sent to Italy. In command of eighty officers and N.C.O.s, from all units of the division, I was sent to Italy for battle experience. We were attached to units corresponding to our own, first with the 4th Indian Division on the Adriatic front, and then with the 8th Indian Division during the break-through after the third battle of Cassino. There is no better training than experience in battle, and those divisions set an inspiring example, though much was also to be learnt from the Germans, who were expert and stubborn fighters.

Just when we were expecting the 6th Division to follow and join us, our hopes were dashed, for with the impending invasion of France, the Allies decided to stop the build up of troops in Italy. The move of the division did not take place, and the advance party returned to Paiforce.

After our high expectations, another summer in Persia was a setback. Through the hills north of Awaz, M.G. Dogras was detailed to guard the railway carrying lend-lease supplies to Russia. The battalion was split up in 32 posts along the track for protection against saboteurs, but the real enemies were boredom and heatstroke. In the bare narrow valleys of solid rock the shade temperatures reached 130°F, and for the first time we had a high sick rate.

Spirits rose when our Divisional Commander, Major-General B. H. Chappel paid us a visit in mid-July. He informed us that the battalion would probably move to Burma, and should begin to train for jungle warfare. This extract from the battalion digest written by me at the time describes the reaction. 'Since the Divisional Commander's visit we have begun to train for jungle warfare. There is not a tree in sight, but this does not disconcert the Indian Army. Have we not spent much of our service training for mountain warfare in the plains, with red flags representing hills and yellows flags marking valleys? We now say to the Dogra, "Imagine a dense jungle of trees, with visibility of only ten yards". He looks at the bare valley and hills and opens his eyes in wonder. However, always willing to play his part, with fixed bayonet and finger on the trigger, he creeps stealthily forward over the bare ground, looking up into imaginary trees for a Japanese sniper.'

That training was entrusted to the second-in-command, Major H. F. Parker, as I had to leave and temporarily command 27th Indian Infantry Brigade with headquarters at Durud. Frank Parker was the only member of the unit with experience of war against the Japanese. When the 5th Dogras was cut off in Burma, though wounded, he was one of their few British officers who managed to swim the River Sittang and escape to fight again. On 1 October, when I rejoined the battalion it was boarding the troopship *Jaladurga* at Basra, bound for India.

Returning to their homeland, with the prospect of seeing their families after two and a half years, the men were in high spirits. Their happiness was evident from much singing of Dogra folk songs, for which small parties from the same village or district gathered round an accompanying drummer. After baking in places such as Talehzang and Tangihaft, they naturally looked forward to seeing their dear ones in the green foothills of the Himilayas. Ten days at sea did much to restore the men's health.

By mid-October we were back in Jullundur with the Dogras streaming home on 28 days' leave, but they had expected 60 days after so long abroad, and were very disappointed. Elsa was still working at Northern Command Headquarters in Rawalpindi, but now wearing the uniform of a Junior Commander of the Women's Auxiliary Corps (India), being one of the first to join when the corps was raised. This meant that she had to get official leave to spend a month with me in Jullundur, following which I managed a fortnights' leave in Rawalpindi, which passed too quickly.

In Jullundur our time was taken up with arranging the men's leave, assembling a Burma scale of equipment, and intensive jungle training. In the open Punjab plain the jungle was again

I

imaginary. Hunting around the Dogra Regimental Centre I recognised a few fine young V.C.O.s and N.C.O.s, and persuaded Colonel Hall to exchange them with some of our older members. We also agreed to exchange Subedar Majors. Shankar Singh was too old for field service, but would do well at the Centre, whereas Sher Singh was younger and ideally suited for an active battalion. He and I had grown up together in the 2nd Dogras, and I knew his sterling qualities.

It was jokingly suggested that Army Headquarters might move us on Christmas Day, which surprisingly they did, and after a week in the train we joined the 5th Indian Division at Jorhat in North Assam. That veteran division had fought in the battle of Keren in Eritrea, and in the early battles of the Western Desert. When the Japanese threat developed it returned to India, and was the only Indian division to fight in both the west and the east.

The division was resting after 14 months of continuous fighting, first in Arakan, and later in the decisive battle of Imphal and the pursuit of the Japanese to the River Chindwin. It was now reorganising to take part in the long strategic moves, which would encircle the Japanese Army in Burma and complete its destruction. In the division was the senior Dogra battalion, the 1st, and we hoped to live up to its high reputation.

While the remainder of the division needed rest, we could not afford to lose the last opportunity of improving our jungle training, which for the first time could be done realistically in a wood near by. As the division had not previously possessed a machine gun battalion and was curious about us, we were asked to give demonstrations in the use of our weapons. These met with the approval of critical veterans, which added to our confidence.

During our stay at Jorhat the 14th Army advanced from the River Chindwin to the Irrawaddy. This great river was then crossed south-west of Mandalay, and the Japanese Army to the north cut off by the capture of Meiktila on 4 March 1945, by the 17th Indian Division under Major-General D. T. Cowan. The 5th Division under Major-General E. C. R. Mansergh had a vital rôle in the next phase of the campaign, and the hour of truth had at last arrived for the M.G. Dogras.

Meiktila was the main Japanese road and rail junction, and its capture threw them into confusion. Taking advantage of this, General Sir William Slim planned a lightning advance to Rangoon, which was to be carried out by the 5th and 17th Divisions of the 4th Corps under Lt.-General Sir Frank Messervy.

The long and difficult supply road from India, and the speed of the advance, meant that the two divisions would have to be maintained by air, which depended on the capture of successive airstrips and airfields. Both divisions were therefore organised each with one airborne brigade, and two motorised brigades. The task of the road element was to seize the next airfield, and that of the air element to fly in and protect it, so that supply aircraft could land. To maintain momentum the two divisions would leapfrog, each leading in turn. When the leading division was fully extended, the one following would pass through and continue the attack, thus relieving the other to collect itself and prepare for the next leapfrog. The plan worked perfectly.

The road element of the 5th Division (123rd and 161st Brigades) left Jorhat in relays between 5 and 18 March to concentrate at Kamye east of the Irrawaddy, covering over 700 miles in 9 days. The airborne element (9th Brigade), including our 'A' Company under Major W. R. Thorp, went ahead by air to reinforce the 17th Division, which was fighting desperately to hold Meiktila against fierce Japanese counter-attacks.

The long road journey was most interesting, though the splendid views were somewhat spoilt by a cloud of choking dust as we drove almost bumper to bumper. The battlefields we passed near Kohima and Imphal marked the scenes of many fierce encounters, which had turned the tide. Kohima will always be remembered for the successful and heroic stand by 4th Bn. Queen's Own Royal West Kent Regiment, when that place was besieged for a fortnight, and repeatedly attacked by the 31st Japanese Division. Beyond Imphal to the Chindwin the road, no more than a dirt track, traversed a mountainous region of wild, almost uninhabited forests. On the far bank of the river, near the crossing at Kalewa, was poignant evidence of our retreat from Burma; the rusty shells of hundreds of abandoned motor vehicles, which refugees and the retreating army could take no further. We crossed the Chindwin again at Monywa, and finally the Irrawaddy at Myitche.

The concentration of the road element at Kamye took place without a hitch. To be poised for battle was no new experience for the veteran 5th Division, but it was for men of the M.G. Dogras, who were anxious to get over the first ordeal. To isolate Meiktila the Japanese had re-occupied the Taungtha Hills, but they were not in great strength and easily cleared. For the first time I saw our Vickers machine guns in action. Such quick firing weapons took a heavy toll on both sides, and the lifeless bodies of fine young men were always a distressing sight; but the battle-field is no place for being squeamish, either you kill or are killed.

Information was coming through of bitter fighting at Meiktila, and I wondered anxiously how Richard Thorp and 'A' Company were faring. The road element reached Meiktila on 31 March, and from many I heard glowing accounts of the courage of the Dogra machine gunners in the battle which had only just ended. I wasted no time in visiting our posts, of which the first was commanded by Havildar Wakil Singh. Proudly he pointed to two derelict Japanese tanks fifty yards in front of his post, grim evidence of the battle he had fought. On the spot I wrote the battalion's first citation for gallantry, which is given below. Wakil Singh was awarded the I.D.S.M. (Indian Distinguished Service Medal).

'On the night 24–25 March 1945 the M.G. Section commanded by No. 7462 Hav. Wakil Singh was astride the road Meiktila-Wundwin, milestone 339·2, on the Meiktila perimeter. After heavy shelling the enemy attacked his position with three tanks and infantry at 2000 hours. Waiting until the attackers were close he opened accurate fire which drove the infantry to ground, and made the tanks close down. Later the tanks attacked alone supported by the fire of the infantry. Opening fire with his M9 grenade discharger he damaged one tank. That again stopped the attack, and eventually the damaged tank was towed away.

Two hours later the remaining two tanks attacked. One M.G. pit received a direct hit, which put the gun out of action and wounded all the crew. One tank penetrated and overran the section position, and as by then all M9 grenades had been fired the section had no anti-tank weapon. The Havildar and his men attacked the tanks with hand grenades and drove them back, while the remaining M.G. continued to pin the enemy infantry to the ground. The enemy finally withdrew at 0400 hours, after a struggle that had lasted for eight hours. At daylight 21 Jap bodies were counted in front of the section position. Throughout the action Hav. Wakil Singh showed leadership and courage of the highest order.'

After I had visited all the posts of 'A' Company, and heard their accounts of the battle, I felt confident that I need have no further anxiety about the performance of our Dogras. On hearing of the exploits of 'A' Company, the other three companies were determined to do as well, and succeeded. During the dash to Rangoon and later in Java the battalion won 15 decorations for bravery, and 30 mentions in despatches, with brave acts like Wakil Singh's often repeated. The unit was normally split up, with a platoon attached to each infantry battalion, and so in every battle fought by the division at that time Dogra machine gunners took part. Their history is therefore interwoven with that of the 5th Division, ably recorded in *Ball of Fire**. A red ball of fire was our proud divisional sign, worn as shoulder flashes by every man.

Of the many events that took place on the way to Rangoon there is space to mention only a few. While we were in Meiktila the 4th Dogras with the 20th Division had reached Wundwin near by, and a party under Major John Frost came across to meet the 1st and M.G. Battalions. For the Dogras it was an historic meeting; three Dogra battalions were on their way to avenge and rescue the three battalions lost in Malaya and Burma.

During the advance information was received that units of the Indian National Army would be encountered on our front, and we wondered how our men would react when faced by their own

* *Ball of Fire* by Antony Brett-James, Gale & Polden, Aldershot, 1951.

kith and kin, but that awkward situation was happily resolved by the I.N.A. surrendering without a fight. I was surprised to see about two thousand of those men, after their surrender, sitting in a long column beside the road. Wearing light khaki, prewar Indian Army uniforms with turbans, they were easily distinguishable from our men, then in jungle green with berets or steel helmets. They looked very ashamed of themselves, and with good cause, for they had been doubly disloyal, first to their own side and then to the Japanese.

Seeing a group of Dogras I went over and talked to them, and formed the impression that they had been confused and subverted by a small group of turncoat I.C.O.s who, convinced the British would lose the war, had cast in their lot with the Japanese. Disillusionment came when the Japanese were on the run. If during captivity British officers had been able to keep in touch with their V.C.O.s and men, I believe the I.N.A. would never have materialised.

The early crushing defeats of the British and Americans had created a super-soldier image of the Japanese, but that did not last. Both British and Indian troops had at last got the measure of the enemy, and were attacking with skill and determination, which were most impressive. To their credit, if cornered the Japs fought to the last man, but they were ready to make an undignified retreat.

The scarcity of prisoners was a serious drawback in obtaining information, and we were urged to make a special effort to bring in live Japs. One morning I saw two men approaching. carrying what looked like a struggling animal. As we were on half rations I thought they had caught a goat or a pig for the pot, but on drawing near I recognised Lieutenant D. H. Jones and his orderly, carrying a protesting Jap who refused to walk. Grabbed by a patrol searching off the road, his only desire was to be shot. David Jones, who had done the grabbing, dumped him on the ground, and with a broad grin said, "Sir, let me present you with your first Jap." Later he was joined in the P.O.W. cage by another prisoner, whose companionship soon helped him to recover from panic and a desire for suicide.

Near Pegu Captain Bill Adams, the Quartermaster, rushed into my headquarters, and said that a Dogra colonel had been rescued down the road. The first person for whom I intended to look on reaching Rangoon was my old friend Henry Power, taken prisoner with the 5th Battalion, and as I raced along in my jeep I felt that the rescued colonel must be Henry; he was. The Japs had endeavoured to march 400 British and American prisoners from Rangoon jail towards the Sittang, but had been intercepted by the speed of our advance.

Like most Japanese P.O.W.s Henry looked starved and a shadow of his former self. He also had both feet heavily bandaged, but was in high spirits and overjoyed at being free. Lesley, his wife, and three daughters had waited anxiously three and a half years for his return. Tragically just before their rescue the prisoners had been bombed by our own aircraft, and the senior officer, Brigadier Hobson, killed.

In the final approach to Rangoon the 17th Division took over the lead. It was the only division that had taken part in both the retreat from Burma and the return, and so to enter Rangoon first was an honour that it deserved. At the last moment it was deprived of this by the seaborne landing of the 26th Indian Division, which found the Japanese had gone. On 6 May the two divisions met at Hlegu just north of Rangoon.

Meanwhile the 5th Division was given the task of securing the west bank of the River Sittang east of Waw in order to intercept the fleeing Japanese. Against our Sittang salient the Japanese made constant counter-attacks to assist their troops endeavouring to escape from the Pegu Yomas to the east. In May and June the mopping up of escaping parties continued. A heavy toll was taken of the Imperial Japanese Army now in full flight, but operations were difficult and exhausting in torrential monsoon rain with the country inundated.

On one of my visits to the salient I walked into a bombardment by Jap heavy mortars, and decided to make for the cover of the nearest machine gun post, which had been dug into a clump of bamboo. To my surprise I found the gun crew sitting outside their trench, and asked Havildar Dalip Singh whether he was trying to get his men killed. He replied with a grin, 'No sahib, there is a large snake hiding in the bamboo, and we prefer to risk the mortars'. That evening Dalip reported, 'We have killed the snake, a large cobra, and all is well'.

Later in the salient, at Nyaungkashe, the Japanese almost surrounded the 4/8th Gurkha Rifles and some of our machine gunners, who, to avoid being cut off, were ordered to withdraw at night. Soon after the withdrawal began the tail of the column lost distance and became separated from the main body. Richard Thorp, who was following at the rear, found himself in command of a group of Gurkhas, a section of Dogras, eleven wounded on stretchers and many walking wounded. All night the party struggled to carry and help the wounded to safety, over nine miles of flooded country with deep water channels, and with the constant fear of walking into the enemy. By great courage, endurance and a miracle all the wounded were brought to safety. For that and other gallant actions Richard was awarded the Military Cross.

For the M.G. Dogras the war in Burma ended triumphantly with some machine guns sited across the Sittang, where the 5th Battalion had met its cruel fate in February 1942. The battalion had acquitted itself with honour and its reputation was high, which gave me deep satisfaction, but it was disappointing not to have been in tactical command of a battle. Had I taken the 6th, an infantry battalion, on service, I should have had the opportunity that never came my way with the machine guns. In battle my task was no more than to move men and guns where required in support of the infantry, and to advise on their use. That was far short of a tactical command for which I had been trained.

The victory in Burma was celebrated by a parade in Rangoon, at which the salute was taken by the Supreme Commander, Admiral Lord Louis Mountbatten. Each division in the 14th Army was represented by a composite battalion, which included parties from all units in the division. I had the honour to command the battalion representing the 5th Indian Division, and have never seen a finer body of men, drawn from all parts of Britain and India (which then included Pakistan).

At the end of June the division was withdrawn from operations and concentrated at Mingaladon, north of Rangoon, to train for a landing in Malaya. We had completed our training in combined operations, and were receiving the final briefing for the landing, when on 6 August the first atom bomb was dropped on Hiroshima; another followed on the 9th at Nagasaki, and the war was over. Instead of embarking for a hazardous landing, we did so for a happier destination, Singapore.

One of the first to land, I set out to look at the area which the battalion was to occupy, and passed a column of British P.O.W.s slowly and painfully marching to meet the ships. They were trying to whistle a march, and carried at the head of the column a small Union Jack. All looked very emaciated, and many were suffering from beri-beri or tropical sores. Dressed in rags, they nevertheless marched in step and straight lines, with their heads high. It was difficult to understand the Japanese, who had marred their fine reputation as soldiers by gross inhumanity. An enormous Japanese rice dump was located in our area, but rather than feed the prisoners they had allowed much of the rice to rot.

At the first opportunity I visited the P.O.W. camps, but of the British officers of the 2nd and 3rd Battalions found only Captain Hector McLean. Apparently after work on the Burma railway he alone returned to Singapore, while the others were kept in Siam. He stayed with us for a few days, and I shall always remember his joy at being free and at facing a square meal. Of the Dogras there were many, notably the two Subedar-Majors Gian Chand and Diwan Chand, and I arranged for them to live with us until repatriated. We had long talks, and although bitter about the cruelty of the Japs, they were far more vehement in their condemnation of those who had turned traitor and joined the I.N.A. Their favourite topic was home, and they longed to hear what had happened in their absence.

The battalion spent September on the island restoring order in the dock area, and then moved to Kota Tinggi on the mainland, the civil headquarters of a district. With comfortable accommodation, it was just the place to recover from the war, and we hoped to be left in peace; but it lasted only a month.

To help clean up the area we were allotted a hundred Japanese prisoners of war, which enabled us to observe our late adversaries at close quarters, working under semi-peaceful conditions. Most of them were short, strongly built, and somewhat overweight on captured food. Always leaving their camp clean and tidy, they worked hard and intelligently, obviously tried to make a good impression, and succeeded in doing so. With their discipline and capacity for work I felt certain that the Japanese would soon recover from the war. We treated them correctly with accommodation in a reasonable camp and full rations, and received no complaints.

At the end of October a serious situation developed in Java. On the 25th, the 49th Indian Infantry Brigade landed at Sourabaya to disarm and evacuate the Japanese, and to rescue Dutch and other internees. The brigade received a hostile reception from the Indonesians, who had declared a republic, and were determined not to return to Dutch rule. Delay in the arrival of British troops had given them $2\frac{1}{2}$ months since the end of the war to raise an army of sorts, equipped and trained by the Japanese, who after handing over their weapons withdrew into the interior.

The British had no desire to enter into local politics or to start another war, and Brigadier A. W. Mallaby endeavoured to win over the co-operation of the Indonesian leaders, and to carry out his mission peacefully. Many thousands of internees were held in camps and prisons in and around the town, and in trying to rescue and transport them to the docks the small British force became dispersed and vulnerable. Taking advantage of that the Indonesians suddenly and treacherously attacked isolated parties of Indian troops, who suffered nearly 400 casualties. Mallaby was murdered by the mob while trying to arrange a truce.

With 12,000 armed Indonesians in possession of Sourabaya more troops were needed to carry out the rescue mission, and the 5th Division was ordered to proceed there. Due to a shortage of ships the M.G. Battalion crossed the Java Sea in small landing craft, packed like sardines, and after a voyage lasting five days arrived at Sourabaya on 7 November. On the voyage we nearly lost Havildar Bachittar, who in the dark fell off a narrow deck into the sea. The sailors reacted immediately, and within a few minutes the six landing craft were moving in a circle, sweeping with searchlights. Not until dawn, more than an hour later, was Bachittar spotted and picked up, to our intense relief; a lucky escape from a shark infested sea, thanks to the Royal Navy.

General Mansergh was very patient in trying to come to terms with the Indonesians, but their new army commanders, strutting about with Japanese swords, were bent on military glory. Having ambushed and killed isolated parties of 49th Brigade their appetite had been whetted. Failing to get agreement, the British had no choice but to advance from the dock area, clear the town and rescue the internees. Our troops were forbidden to fire unless fired on, but were met by a hail of bullets and the fighting began.

Clearing the town street by street was a slow and costly operation which lasted 19 days. At first the Indonesians fought bravely, but were no match for our veterans, and after a few days invariably ran when attacked. Even so our losses mounted.

During one of these encounters I heard that Havildar Munshi's section near by had suffered casualties and that he had been killed. To deal with the situation Lieutenant George Shipley and I edged towards the gun position, dodging from house to house to avoid enemy fire. The houses appeared to be deserted, but one was obviously occupied, and I shouted asking if anyone was at home, whereupon three Dutch women and a small boy emerged from a cellar. They were delighted to see us, and said that the enemy soldiers had only just left. As the wives of doctors forced to treat the Indonesians, they had escaped internment, and been allowed to live in that house. I arranged for their protection until the return of their husbands, who had been made to accompany the Indonesian troops; luckily all survived. I called those ladies the front-line girls, and they gave me a much valued parting gift of silver inscribed, 'Sourabaya 25.11.45 Front-line girls.'

Thousands of Dutch and other nationals were rescued from prison camps and gradually shipped home. Convoys of lorries crammed with fine-looking Dutch people, waving and cheering, were daily driven down to the ships. Their departure marked the end of an empire.

Sporadic fighting continued until April 1946, when Dutch troops took over, and the 5th Division returned to India. The loss of life in Java seemed unnecessary, and was deeply deplored. Veterans and heroes of Eritrea, the Western Desert, Imphal and Burma were killed in a futile conflict which was forced on us. The M.G. Battalion incurred 40 casualities, and other units many more.

When the 1st and M.G. Battalions sailed from Sourabaya it was at last the end of the Second World War for the Dogra Regiment. After six years of war the regiment was stronger than ever, with three veteran battalions in the forefront, two hardened on the north-west frontier ready to take the field, and two fit for upgrading from garrison to active status. The will and capacity to fight on remained, but all rejoiced at victory and the end of human sacrifice. The Dogras could be proud of their record and battle honours, which are still revered in the Dogra Regiment of the new Indian Army.

On my return to India Elsa was demobilised, with two medals as a memento of her war service. So after six years we unpacked our boxes to set up home; alas! the best Persian rug had been devoured by white ants. My first job could not have been more agreeable, to reconstitute my parent battalion the 2nd which had been captured in Singapore, and to amalgamate the 2nd and 6th Battalions. From the survivors of the 2nd only 4 V.C.O.s and 101 men were fit and willing to serve on, so most came from the 6th which I had commanded for five years and knew so well.

Lt.-Colonel J. W. Middleton similarly amalgamated the 3rd Battalion, also captured at Singapore, and the 7th. It was a moving experience for those present when the 2nd and 3rd Dogras marched again, and the gaps in the regiment were filled.

On leaving the 2nd Battalion I commanded the Dogra Regimental Centre until Independence Day. Normally in a regiment an officer commanded only one of the battalions or the regimental centre for four years, but due to the war I commanded the 6th, M.G. and 2nd Battalions and the Centre successively for nine years, perhaps an Indian Army record and a wonderful experience.

At the end of the war all the indications were that India would soon gain her independence. During the Raj the Dogras had generally kept out of politics, but by 1947, after a hundred years of tutelage, they were ready for freedom, which they believed had been won on the battlefields of the Western Desert, Italy and Burma, and not by politicians trying to sabotage the war effort in India. In the future control of their country the Dogra Rajputs intended to have a voice, and their views were made clear to me at the Centre, when we happened to be discussing a very different subject, the use of regimental funds.

The Dogras said that in their community the British had taken over power from the Rajputs, who then had remained loyal to the Raj, especially in the armed forces and in time of war; but that had not made the Dogra Rajputs rich. The people who had accumulated great wealth during British rule were the Brahmans and Banias (traders), who were therefore able to educate their sons at British and Indian universities. Prior to the Raj these people had been kept in their own spheres, as priests, advisers and merchants, but by engaging in politics and acquiring superior education, they would now rule.

Only by improving their education could the Dogra Rajputs hope to regain their traditional influence.

The private funds of the Centre had increased over the years, and been considerably augmented at the end of the war by the funds of disbanded battalions. The future use of that money was under discussion, and I was advised by the I.C.O.s and V.C.O.s to put as much as possible into a scholarship fund for the sons of soldiers of the regiment, which I was very glad to arrange. The fund was organised by a very fine old officer, Captain Harjallu Singh, and I hear has been a great success.

Apart from a change in their officers, independence would make little difference in the lives of the V.C.O.s and men, and they approached the event calmly. For the I.C.O.s the prospects were far more exciting; although mostly junior and inexperienced, they could expect rapid promotion. In numbers they were now adequate for the peace-time armies of both India and Pakistan. Their impatience to take over was natural, and they exerted all possible pressure to expedite the departure of British officers. They had their way, and nearly all were replaced at the time they were most needed, when a violent communal war broke out after independence with appalling losses. Only British officers, with their experience and influence on both sides, could have prevented that conflict from getting out of control. It would have been wiser to have replaced them more gradually.

BOOK TWO

1947

*End of the British Raj
and Tragedy in the Punjab*

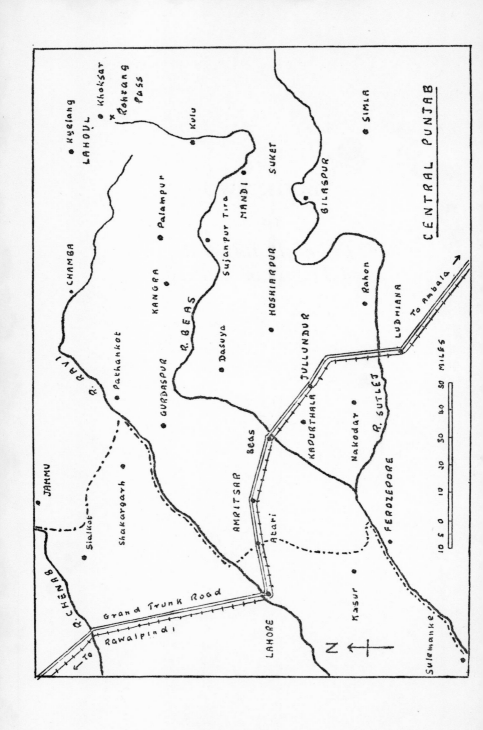

CENTRAL PUNJAB

9. At the start of a day's march, Lahoul, 1939

10. Buddhist Lamas in dance dress, Lahoul

11. F.M. Sir Claude Auchinleck meets officers M.G. Bn. Dogra Regiment, Rangoon, 1945 (Subedar Major Sher Singh third from right)

12. General Sir Douglas Gracey presents the Indian Order of
Merit to Subedar Ranbir Singh, a hero of Nunshigam

13. First reunion dinner of the Dogra Regiment after the Second World War, Jullundur, 1946

14. Gulmarg Golf Club, 1947, just before Independence

15. Motor convoy of evacuees moving to Pakistan, 1947

16. Evacuee train, 1947

CHAPTER VI

INDEPENDENCE AND THE COMMUNAL WAR

In March 1947, Rear-Admiral Viscount Mountbatten of Burma came to India as Viceroy to hand over rule by June 1948. When he announced that India and Pakistan would become separate independent countries on 15 August 1947, there was great surprise that it should happen so soon. The division of the Punjab caused grave concern to the Hindus and Sikhs west of the new boundary and to the Muslims east of it, as attacks on them, even before Independence, showed that they were in deadly peril.

The people most likely to react fiercely to partition were the six million Sikhs, of whom a third would be isolated in Pakistan, where they were rich in land and property. The Sikhs felt that the splitting of their small nation was a threat to its survival. The danger to those in Pakistan became clear when, beginning in March, Muslims killed many Sikhs in Lahore, Rawalpindi, Multan and other places, burned their homes and *gurdwaras* (temples), and further insulted their religion by setting light to their beards. A particularly brutal and provocative act was the burning of a famous *guardwara* in Lahore with twenty people inside. The Sikhs are the most militant and turbulent race in India, and the events that followed in the East Punjab were dominated by their desire for revenge, and determination to unite east of the boundary.

The Dogras were also affected by partition though not as seriously as the Sikhs. A small minority lived west of the boundary in the area Sialkot-Shakargarh, and in the Canal Colonies south-west of Lahore. The future of Jammu and Kashmir was uncertain, but comfort was drawn from the fact that the ruling prince, Maharaja Sir Hari Singh, was a Dogra Rajput. As confidently expected he eventually decided to accede to India.

On 23 August 1947, I became responsible for security in the civil districts of Jullundur and Hoshiarpur, and for a few weeks in Ludhiana. The three districts, together with those of Kangra and Ferozepore, formed the Jullundur Civil Division. The two senior officials in the division had been British until 7 August, when they were relieved by Hindus; Mr. I. E. Jones the Commissioner by Mr. J. M. Shrinagesh, and Mr. D. Gainsford the Deputy Inspector General of Police (D.I.G.) by Mr. S. R. Chaudri. About the same time in the districts any British or Muslim Deputy Commissioners and Superintendents of Police were replaced by Hindus or Sikhs.

Jullundur and Hoshiarpur Districts were in an area known as the Jullundur Doab, land of two rivers, situated in the centre of the Sikh homeland. The Doab was about sixty miles long and wide, and bounded by the River Beas to the west and north, foothills of the Himalayas to the east, and the River Sutlej to the south. Hoshiarpur District covered the north and east, Jullundur District the centre and south, and the Princely State of Kapurthala the west. State troops were independently responsible for internal security in Kapurthala, but help was given by the regular brigade in Jullundur when needed.

The three main communities in the Doab and Ludhiana District were Sikhs, Muslims and Hindus, of whom the last were divided into Punjabi Hindus and Dogras. These communities were distributed throughout the area, except the Dogras who were concentrated in the foothills.

The population of the Doab was about three millions, of whom about 41 per cent were Muslims, 22 per cent Sikhs and the rest mostly Hindus. The figures for Ludhiana District were; total nearly one million, 37 per cent Muslims, 42 per cent Sikhs. In the three main towns the inhabitants approximately numbered; Jullundur City and Ludhiana City 120,000 each, Hoshiarpur Town 40,000. In both cities nearly two-thirds of the people were Muslims, and in Hoshiarpur Town nearly half were Muslims.

In the whole area the Muslims were mostly poor tenant farmers, who, even where stronger in number, were over-awed by the more powerful Sikhs, of whom many were tenants. Very different in character were the Muslims of the West Punjab, who were robust and warlike. In the East Punjab they were loosely held together by the Muslim League, but lacked an effective militant organisation, which became very apparent after Indepence, when the Sikhs began to exterminate them.

The Punjabi Hindus were mostly urban people, bankers, merchants and shopkeepers, who owned much of the wealth. Because of their affluence they were the best educated, and as members of the Congress Party very active politically. Although strongly hostile to the Muslims, they were not anxious to join in the violence, and took little part in the massacres; the Sikhs needed no assistance, nor were they disposed to share the spoils.

Described in earlier chapters, the Dogras were an agricultural people, who preferred to segregate in their own villages in the foothills, whereas the Sikhs and Muslims inhabited the flat plains. In revenge for the killing of their people in Pakistan, the Dogras took part in the slaughter of Muslims in Hoshiarpur District, though not as systematically or ruthlessly as the Sikhs. They certainly showed more respect for women and children.

Sandwiched between Muslims and Hindus, the small Sikh nation had survived only by cohesion and better organisation, founded on their religious, political and military brotherhood. Mostly farmers living on rich productive land, physically they were the finest race in India. Their political party, organised on military lines and grouped in *jathas* (legions), was called the Akalis (Immortals) after the famous shock troops of Maharaja Ranjit Singh. Many ex-servicemen provided a trained nucleus, and acted as experienced leaders. The *gurdwaras* were not only houses of worship, but also military headquarters, of which the chief was the Golden Temple of Amritsar.

In the Doab, even in peace time, it was a common sight to see *jathas* marching in military formation from *gurdwara* to *gurdwara* singing militant songs. With some in ancient uniforms and all carrying *kirpans,* they looked like mediaeval soldiers marching to battle, though officially they were participating in religious processions, with which the authorities did not interfere. That private army was never more ready than in August 1947, and the holy *kirpan* was used in shameful atrocities.

With the many murders in 1947 before Independence, both in the East and West Punjab, the planners in Delhi must have been aware that a major communal conflict would follow Independence; police intelligence must have known of the preparations in the *gurdwaras* and elsewhere. Top priority should have been given to ensuring that all the security forces would be effective, consisting not only of troops, but also of police and magistrates. The only way to control the situation was by the quick arrest of those organising murder, a task for the police and not the army. The planners had not done their job well, for the Punjab Police began to disintegrate on the first day of Independence.

The withdrawal of British troops was a wise decision. Their intervention in the Communal War would have brought them into conflict with both sides, and wherever used they would have been accused of partiality and made the scapegoats. Also their involvement would have defeated the object of handing over rule and withdrawing. However, there had to be a British rearguard, and the right choice was made; the British officers of the Indian Army. They knew the people and were trusted on both sides, which made them invaluable as organisers and mediators. Thanks to the loyalty of their men they could move about with reasonable safety, and rarely became targets for the mob. Unfortunately that rearguard was not as strong as it could have been.

On 15 August 1947, the day India and Pakistan celebrated their independence, I vacated command of the Dogra Regimental Centre, and was appointed to command Jullundur Sub-Area, which included the Jullundur garrison, and the regimental centres of the 1st, 4th and 7th Gurkha Rifles at Dharmsala, Bakloh and Palampur respectively. The normal internal security role of the Sub-Area had been taken over by the Punjab Boundary Force, especially formed under Major-General T. W. Rees to deal with a threatening situation.

The Boundary Force, totalling 55,000 troops, had its head-quarters at Lahore, and was disposed either side of the new boundary in the Punjab. It consisted of local units reinforced by the veteran 4th Indian Division, which had become famous in Eritrea, the Western Desert and Italy. The 11th Indian Infantry Brigade under Brigadier G. T. Wheeler had moved into Jullundur Sub-Area, where all operational troops were placed under his command. As Sub-Area Commander I remained responsible mainly for administration, and various training establishments, such as the Dogra Regimental Centre in Jullundur, and the three Gurkha Regimental Centres in the Kangra Hills.

On the morning of the 15th I attended a ceremonial parade of the Dogra Regimental Centre, at which the new national flag of India was blessed by the Pandit, raised, saluted and cheered. That night in the Centre a celebration dinner was given for all ranks, followed by a concert with patriotic scenes, such as children on the stage waving the new tricolour and singing. The following night there was another dinner for officers, to which senior persons in the station were invited. Nearly all those present were Indians, and naturally there was much excitement and rejoicing. Only a few British officers remained, but we entered into the spirit of the occasion, and conveyed our best wishes for the future of India and the regiment.

In Jullundur Cantonment the Independence celebrations were a happy event, but in nearby Lahore and Amritsar they took the form of hate and savagery. In Lahore the Muslims began to burn *gurdwaras* and slaughter Hindus and Sikhs. The latter not to be outdone paraded Muslim girls and women naked through the streets of Amritsar, raped them, and hacked them to death. From the Golden Temple the Akali leader Master Tara Singh exhorted the Sikhs to eliminate the Muslims, and received a ready response. The Sikh prayer, "First of all I worship thee, O sword", was now given full expression.

With the two capital cities of the East and West Punjab showing the way the trouble was certain to spread. Out of 8,000 British officers 2,800 had agreed to remain until the end of the year, primarily to assist with the division of the army, and its reconstitution into the two separate armies of India and Pakistan. Our task proved to be quite different and far less congenial.

The first serious attack by the Sikhs in the Doab took place on the night of 31 July, against a Muslim village called Jhand, in which 14 Muslims were killed and the outskirts of the village set on fire. As the British Raj still existed, the Muslims were not demoralised, fought back bravely, and saved themselves and their village. The two senior police officers, D.I.G. and Superintendent, were British, and normal procedures of law and order were immediately put into effect. Adjoining villages were searched, attackers identified and arrested, and steps taken to bring them to trial.

Had all the first attacks been dealt with in the same way the situation could have been controlled, but that was the last time British justice and impartiality prevailed. Within the next few days the remaining British officials and police officers were replaced, and their departure greatly reduced the chances of survival of the Muslims, for the new administration showed little interest in protecting them. The rot began with a farcical internal security conference.

That conference took place on Independence Day. At such meetings the local heads of the administration, police and army decided on measures to maintain law and order. In the past members of the conference had been British, Hindu, Sikh and Muslim, and had observed strict impartiality towards all communities. After the departure of the British and Muslim officials, except for Brigadier Wheeler and myself the members were entirely Hindu and Sikh, headed by the new Commissioner and D.I.G. of Police.

The Indian members expressed concern about the use of Muslim troops, and insisted that they should not be located in Jullundur City, where the majority of the inhabitants were Muslims. Members felt that these, encouraged by the presence of their own troops, might begin disturbances, which could even threaten the security of Civil Lines close by, where officials had their homes and offices. Wheeler and I disagreed strongly and pointed out that the Muslims, finding themselves on the wrong side of the boundary, were terrified and the last to make trouble, whereas the Sikhs were poised for attack, and nothing would encourage them more than the absence of Muslim troops. We were overruled; there was worse to come.

The next decision of the conference was even more fatal. The D.I.G. stated that Muslim police had proved unreliable in the Amritsar fighting, and failed to protect non-Muslims, which was confirmed by other members who had been in that city. After their graphic descriptions of Hindus and Sikhs being killed while Muslim police looked on, mistrust of them was understandable. The meeting decided to disarm the Muslim police of the Jullundur Civil Division, which virtually meant their disbandment, for without weapons they were not prepared to face suicide against Sikh *jathas*, and refused to serve.

Disarming, however, was not the main reason for the departure of the Muslim policemen; responsibility for that rested with the planners in Delhi, who had failed to ensure that an impartial mixed police force would survive. Muslim soldiers who gladly remained in the East Punjab to protect their own people, did so only because of mutual trust between officers and men. On Independence when British and Muslim police officers were replaced by Hindus and Sikhs, the position of the Muslim rank and file became untenable, because officers and men did not trust each other.

Had British and Muslim police officers been retained during the crisis period, I believe the men would have served on like the soldiers. The preservation of a mixed force would also have been helped by placing it under command of the army, thus ensuring closer co-ordination and mutual support.

In the Doab the police numbered about 1,600. In the officer and upper subordinate ranks Muslims and non-Muslims were about equal, but in the lower ranks there were many more Muslims than Hindus and Sikhs. The loss of considerably more than half its strength made the force not only very inadequate, but strongly partisan.

Tyrwhitt Wheeler and I had gone to the conference hoping to hear of firm Government action to deal with the threat to peace, such as the police and army rounding up murder gang leaders and seizing arms. Instead, a large part of the security force was disbanded, and the initiative handed over to the *jathas* on a plate. There was little doubt that in Pakistan there had been similar reactions, and so the Communal War was about to begin in earnest.

After getting rid of the Muslims, the police were joined by Hindu and Sikh policemen who had fled for their lives from Pakistan, and arrived with lurid stories of slaughter and atrocities there. Not surprisingly the police became dedicated to the Communal War, and as far as they were concerned murder could be committed with impunity by anyone, provided the victim was a Muslim. Although the Muslims in the Doab were too frightened to make a single aggressive move, the police filled the jails with their leaders, and began a systematic search for their arms; improvised spears, clubs and an occasional shotgun. Their removal was often timed to take place before an attack by the Sikhs.

The local authorities, even if they were not directing the police, certainly failed to curb their activities. As the police were not under its command, the army had no authority to intervene when they deprived the Muslims of their tougher leaders and makeshift weapons so as to make them easy victims. The Sikhs were very much on edge, awaiting the final details of the Radcliffe boundary award, which were not announced until 17 August. That confirmed their worst fears and the next day they struck the first blow.

Jullundur City was about two miles from the Cantonment where the troops were quartered. The 120,000 inhabitants of the City, who were predominantly Muslims, all lived in a labyrinth of narrow streets and lanes. Only about 3,000 Sikhs lived in the City, but on the night of the 18th they poured in from the surrounding villages, and street by street began a massacre of the Muslims. The City was the responsibility of 11th Brigade, but early next morning I went there, accompanied by a staff officer, to see how I could help.

Except for armed gangs of Sikhs the streets were empty, as

surviving Muslims and even Hindus had locked themselves in. Several streets had been sacked and set alight in predominantly Muslim areas, and houses were full of dead bodies. We stopped the car when my companion recognised a Sikh, who had served with him on active service as a havildar, but now clutching a *kirpan* was obviously hunting Muslims. He grinned in a guilty way and was not anxious to talk. Hearing machine gun fire we drove towards it, and on entering a long street saw two tanks of which the leader was firing.

Near the tanks we met an armed police patrol with a hand-cuffed prisoner, and asked what had happened, to which the leader replied that during a search for weapons he had found a shotgun in the house of the prisoner. That patrol could easily have stopped a slaughter of Muslims, which was taking place within a hundred yards, and yet they were moving away from the scene with their prisoner, who we were shocked to find was a Muslim. With a few exceptions that was typical of police behaviour during the crisis.

Beyond the tanks we saw the incendiaries and murderers at work. Armed with *kirpans* and using long poles with burning rags at the top, they were setting alight to Muslim houses, of which the occupants had to choose between dying in the flames or being cut down in the street. To impress me the tank machine gunner fired another burst, which had no effect on the Sikhs, because he was firing high. I asked the V.C.O. in command why the gunner was not firing straight. He replied that the machine gun was intended for anti-aircraft fire and could not be depressed, and he had no shells for the tank gun. I noticed that he and the tank crews were wearing revolvers, and asked why he did not use these weapons, to which he replied that they were inadequate as Sikhs were up in windows with rifles. Obviously he was being evasive and we had reached deadlock; there was an awkward silence.

The Jat soldiers were not unfriendly, but conveyed by their demeanour that the Raj had ended, and the conflict should be left to them to settle in their own way. I ordered my staff officer to fire down the street with his revolver, keeping mine loaded as a precaution. The reaction of the Sikhs was immediate, as, startled, they looked round and then bolted. That incident was a clear indication that Hindu troops could not be relied on to protect Muslims, especially those such as Jats who came from the Punjab. While Hindus recruited outside the Punjab showed less reluctance to act, notably Gurkhas, only Muslim troops were really effective in protecting their own people.

How considerably fewer Sikhs overpowered so many Muslims might appear surprising, yet the explanation is simple. Battles can only be won by attack, but had the Muslims emerged from their houses to concentrate and counter-attack they would have been shot down by the Hindu-Sikh security forces. Of the population only the Hindus and Sikhs could move freely, and so gathered in overwhelming strength to attack one street or one village at a time. The Muslims could only barricade themselves inside, and pray that the rescue troops would arrive before the killers.

The first major attack by the Akalis in Jullundur City was crucial, and had they been given a sharp lesson the result would have been sobering, and probably discouraged further attacks. Surprised and elated by their easy success they became more confident and ambitious, and spread the attacks to Hoshiarpur Town, Ludhiana City and the villages, where the troops were quite inadequate and the Akalis had a wide choice of unprotected targets. Intoxicated by mounting success, they were determined to eliminate the Muslims and to drive them out of the East Punjab.

Operational responsibility in the Doab and Ludhiana District rested with 11th Brigade under Brigadier Wheeler, and to help him I mustered every available man from the training and administrative units in the Sub-Area. The biggest of these, the Dogra Centre, improvised two companies of partially trained recruits, under command of their own instructors.

As Tyrwhitt Wheeler had not elected to serve after Independence, on 23 August, I was ordered to hand over the Sub-Area to Brigadier Lakhindar Singh, and assume command of 11th

Brigade. I had held the appointment of Sub-Area Commander for only eight days. Such rapid changes were typical of the confusion at the time, with the result that commanders and units rarely got to know each other well.

Shortly before departing Wheeler had had a serious altercation with the civil authorities about the police. Following a massacre of Muslims in Hoshiarpur, he visited that town to find the jail full of Muslims for possessing crude weapons, though not a single Hindu or Sikh had been arrested; nor had any been killed. Officers of the Mahar Regiment were furious, and reported that police had been seen helping with the massacre, and had deliberately directed troops to wrong places to prevent them from saving Muslims. Wheeler demanded the removal of the local Sikh police officer, only to be rebuffed. Clearly the army could no longer act by supporting the civil authority; it had to take the lead. There were isolated instances of civil officials and police officers co-operating, but generally they were too obsessed with hatred of Pakistan and the Muslims to do so.

It was a great honour to command the famous 11th Brigade, and to wear the Red Eagle shoulder flashes of 4th Indian Division, to which I had been attached for a few months in Italy. The brigade had been the first to leave India in the Second World War, and had fought from Sidi Barrani in the Western Desert to the Gothic Line in Italy. The two senior staff officers, Major D. Ramsay-Brown the Brigade Major, and Major C. H. Williams the Deputy Assistant Adjutant and Quartermaster General, were highly qualified and experienced. The brigade was scattered in small detachments over a wide area, with which fortunately I was well acquainted, having often crossed the Doab on recruiting trips to the Dogra country to the north. I lost no time in visiting troops and the chief trouble spots, beginning with Jullundur City.

As troops available for the City were very inadequate to protect all the Muslim homes, isolated houses and streets had gradually been vacated, and the Muslims herded together in certain localities or keeps. But where guards were not reliable and prepared to turn a blind eye, even the keeps were attacked by slash and grab gangs, especially at night. Abandoned streets had a wartime appearance, with all houses looted and many reduced to charred walls; a stench of death pervaded the air.

Driving slowly down a deserted street I heard a groan, opened a front door, and found lying in a pool of blood an old Muslim, who had just been shot. He said that he had been shot by the soldiers. A short distance down the street, on protective patrol, was a platoon of Sikhs, and the commander admitted that one of his men had shot the Muslim, because he ran when challenged. As the old man had obviously been shot when cornered in a house, the explanation did not ring true.

The young soldier who had shot the man appeared quite pleased with himself, and with a loaded magazine on his Bren gun only too eager to repeat the act. I gave the Sikhs the usual talk about the duty of the army in India to save Muslims, and in Pakistan to save Hindus and Sikhs, and added that they did not uphold the honour of a famous regiment by killing an old man. They looked very sullen, and I formed the impression that our two Sikh companies would have been far better employed in Pakistan, rescuing their own people.

Soon after that incident I had another warning of the unreliability of Punjabi troops. A platoon of Dogras was protecting a predominantly Muslim village near Jullundur, when it was attacked at night by Sikhs. Nearly every Muslim adult and child in the village was slaughtered and mutilated, as apart from firing a few random shots the troops did nothing. Dogra families fleeing from Pakistan had arrived at the regimental centre for refuge, bringing harrowing stories, which stirred up a desire for revenge, and as a result even the trustworthy Dogras failed to respond on occasions. More often, however, discipline overcame prejudice and they carried out their duty, though without enthusiasm; much depended on the influence of the commander on the spot.

The effectiveness of a brigade depended more on its composition than numbers. Whereas normally the troops were well disciplined and staunch, in that communal conflict their reliability varied considerably, especially when given no clear and firm direction by their new governments. Before assessing the

composition of 11th Brigade it is necessary to consider the reactions of different classes of soldiers, when faced with the
problem of saving Muslims in the East Punjab; with which this
account is concerned. In the West the problem and attitudes
were reversed.

Defending their own people the Muslim troops were inclined
to use maximum rather than minimum force. The Sikhs were
not interested in protecting Muslims at all, and only too eager
to help their own *jathas*. The Hindus varied from acting strongly
to looking the other way; those from the Punjab, who had
suffered from partition of their country and lost homes and
relations in Pakistan, were most reluctant to help Muslims; those
living at a distance from and unaffected by the new border were
more prepared to do their duty, especially men of low caste
like the Mahars, who were not so fanatical about religion.

Officers naturally had a strong influence on the conduct of
their troops, and when a British officer was replaced it tended
to make them more partisan and less reliable. If the new commander was obsessed with a hatred for Muslims, only one hostile
address to his men was enough to change their conception of
duty. Most Hindu and Sikh officers were strongly opposed to
the partition of India, and they became even more enraged
when Pakistan declared itself an Islamic state, and began to
throw out non-Muslims. It was difficult for them to remain impartial.

11th Brigade was composed as follows:

Of the four battalions, the two at the top were veterans
who had served with distinction in 4th Division during the
Second World War, and the others were new with little experience.

3rd (Parachute) Bn. 1st Punjab Regiment—Two companies
   Muslims, one Sikhs, one Rajputs.
3rd Royal Bn. Frontier Force Regiment—Two companies
   Muslims, one Sikhs, one Dogras.
2nd Bn. Bihar Regiment—One company Muslims, three
   Hindus.

3rd Bn. Mahar Regiment—Scheduled (low) caste Hindus.
'C' Squadron 18th Cavalry (Tanks)—Jats.
'B' Squadron Central India Horse (Tanks)—Dogras and Jats.
4th Field Company Engineers—Muslims.
Brigade Defence Platoon—Gurkhas.
Dogra Regimental Centre—Two recruit companies Dogras.

Due to post-war demobilisation the average strength of a battalion was only about 450, so that the brigade was weaker than it appeared on paper. Squadrons or companies by classes numbered, Hindus 13 (5 from the Punjab), Sikhs 2, and Muslims 6. This composition would have been ideal for a brigade operating in Pakistan to save Hindus and Sikhs, where there would have been 15 utterly reliable squadrons or companies, and only 6 reluctant to act. In India reliability was reversed, and in the Doab only 6 really effective Muslim companies (600 men) could not cover a densely populated area of about 3,000 square miles.

The shortage of Muslim troops would have been balanced had the Muslim police been retained. Until Independence both in Jullundur and Hoshiarpur the police superintendents had been British, and over 400 Muslim police in each district under a British officer would have been worth two reliable battalions. Unlike the troops they knew the area intimately, and where to look for the murder gang leaders, which would have enabled the security forces to seize the initiative and arrest them. Unfortunately the loss of the Muslim police and weak Government direction threw us on the defensive, so that we could do no more than rescue the survivors of attack.

The brigade was deployed roughly as follows: Bihars in the north including Jullundur City; Mahars in the east including Hoshiarpur Town; Frontier Force battalion in the south including Ludhiana City; Punjabis in the centre. To the west was Kapurthala with its own state troops and police. Tanks were allotted to battalions and to co-operate with Kapurthala state troops. The Dogra Centre provided guards and patrols in the Cantonment and its vicinity.

On visiting battalion areas, I found the commanders doing their best to save Muslims, but the troops were quite inadequate, and much of the country was unprotected and open to attack. The Sikhs were succeeding too well and acquiring too much loot to listen to reason, and their only response was to demand the withdrawal of Muslim troops, and the banishment of all Muslims to Pakistan. The chief appeal of the Muslims was for their own soldiers to protect them from the *jathas* and the Hindu-Sikh police. It was a desperate situation, but by holding on the army was saving thousands of lives, and preventing an even greater massacre.

One of my first visitors at brigade headquarters was a senior Muslim magistrate living in Hoshiarpur, an elderly cultured man, who said that the slaughter of Muslims in that town had been appalling, and he had seen the police participating, On the night of the first attack blood was pouring from the upper storeys into the streets below. Though the Muslims were concentrated in keeps with Hindu guards, the killing continued, and he implored me to send Muslim soldiers. I visited Hoshiarpur to find that the Mahars were gradually getting the situation under control, at least in the town, though large parts of the district were unprotected.

Similar heart-rending appeals arrived every day; the headman of a village, a retired V.C.O., or someone of importance would make his perilous way in the dark to brigade headquarters, and plead for help before it was too late. I endeavoured to meet those calls, but sometimes the soldiers arrived too late, to find a whole village slaughtered.

As the Sikhs were completely out of hand and showing no respect for women and children, concern was expressed about the safety of British families in Jullundur. British officers found themselves in a most invidious position, for, though not wishing to take sides, they could not stand by while innocent people were being murdered. If their troops refused they took it upon themselves to disperse the killers, which provoked the Sikhs, and Master Tara Singh and his followers began a hate campaign against British officers. In 1/9th Gurkha Rifles, who joined us later, Major M. S. Bradford-Martin was ambushed and killed, and Captain D. St. J. Forrer wounded.

The fears for British women and children were understandable, but I was against any kind of panicky evacuation, and if the situation deteriorated intended to put families in the Dogra Regimental Centre, where they would have been perfectly safe. About twenty families were scattered in bungalows and the two hotels, and I also had to consider whether they should be guarded, but I felt it would be quite wrong to divert men for that purpose, when Muslims all around us were being slaughtered through lack of protection. A few Dogra patrols moved about the Cantonment at night, and I decided they would have to suffice.

When all our Muslim servants fled to Pakistan, Elsa and I had to give up our bungalow and move to the small Jubilee Hotel, where due to the intense heat we slept at night on the verandah. For a few days a Sikh brigadier moved in next door, and also decided to sleep on the verandah. To our surprise we found a Sikh sentry with a rifle and fixed bayonet standing at the foot of his bed, which shows that there was a general feeling of insecurity. We found it difficult to sleep with the noise of changing sentries and rifles butts hitting the hard floor, and after the first night decided to sacrifice this unsought protection and to move round the corner.

Only a week after I joined 11th Brigade, Major Ramsay-Brown was posted as second-in-command of 1/2nd Gurkha Rifles, who were due to join the British Army in Malaya. Of the old staff only Major Williams and Lieutenant J. G. Temple, the Intelligence Officer, remained, and I was thankful to have them at least, particularly Clifford Williams, who would take good care of administration, including transport and supplies, and leave me free to concentrate on operations.

It was left to me to fill the Brigade Major vacancy, and I was lucky to find Captain D. H. Jones at the Dogra Centre awaiting demobilisation and repatriation. He had been with me in the M.G. Battalion during the war, and gallantly agreed to serve on. Although not a trained staff officer he was very competent, and above all possessed good nerves; much needed at that time.

Before the departure of the British civil officials and police officers, intelligence had been good, but broke down immediately they left, and we remained completely in the dark as to Akali intentions. On the other hand the Akalis knew the location of every soldier, whether he was for or against them, thus could always choose gaps in the defences. From units we received reports of attacks and casualties, but rarely any warning.

To help in assessing the situation I used to fly for an hour or two, almost every day, in a small Auster observation aircraft. Each flight covered a large area, and flying at low altitude gave a good view of movement on the ground. Clearly the Muslims were paralysed in their villages or evacuee* camps, while Sikh *jathas* were always on the move, assembling, advancing to attack, or returning loaded with loot. With four battalions deployed I had hoped to see more troops about, but in such a large area detachments were miles apart.

Taking advantage of their freedom to move, the *jathas* concentrated in crushing strength against each Muslim village, or Muslim part of a mixed village, giving the defenders little chance. Even so, considering the probable fate that awaited them, it was surprising that they did not always fight back to the death, for had they done so it would have deterred the Sikhs, helped the rescuers, and probably resulted in fewer losses. The atacks only continued with such confidence because the Akali losses were negligible. On occasions the Muslims did defend themselves with courage, but more often they surrendered and pleaded for mercy.

The lot of those who submitted depended on the whim of the *jathedars*, who sometimes were content to seize their homes, property and young women, execute those on their black list, and turn the rest out into the open. At other times the Muslims were not so fortunate, and were massacred to the last child, as invariably happened when they resisted.

* 'Evacuee' was the term used for anyone leaving, and 'refugee' for anyone entering, either country.

L

Attacks generally followed the same pattern. On Muslim lookouts giving the alarm, men would collect on their low flat rooftops with improvised weapons to protect themselves and their families. A few bursts of fire would bring them down to shelter behind the walls of their courtyards and gardens. Soon forced or frightened back by overwhelming numbers, the defenders would retreat inside their houses and lock the doors. The *jathas* would then break up into parties and deal with each house in turn.

From the air I often saw *jathas* assembling outside a village *gurdwara*, in order to be incited by their political and spiritual leaders before setting out for a bloody mission. It was nauseating to see that these leaders were elderly men with long grey beards, and not irresponsible youths; the killing was not organised by hooligans, but by the patriarchs of the Sikh nation.

Several days passed before I saw an actual attack, or rather the end of one, at a small village near Rahon, north of the River Sutlej. On approaching I saw a *jatha* of a few thousand swarming around the village, and loading loot on to bullock carts. The only survivors appeared to be about a hundred prisoners standing in a straight line as if on parade. On drawing near I was shocked to find that they were young women and girls, being inspected by a group of grey-bearded *jathedars*, at what looked like a distribution ceremony. Several corpses were visible of people obviously cut down while trying to run away, but of the other villagers there was no sign. On the flat open plain with clear visibility for miles, they were not to be seen near the village nor fleeing from it, and were presumably dead in their houses. The women prisoners had probably seen their families slaughtered before their eyes.

The pilot, a fine young Sikh artillery officer, said, "I am ashamed of my people". The only weapon we possessed was my revolver, and he readily agreed to fly low in circles, while I fired and used up my ammunition. He had only a Very signal pistol, of which the Very lights could do little harm, but he fired them as a gesture of disgust. The Sikhs all dived for cover, and when our feeble attack ended a few fired back.

We returned immediately to headquarters, from where I directed the nearest troops to move to the village, but the Sikhs had taken alarm, and wasted no time in fading away into nearby villages. The troops who had several miles to cover, arrived to find only dead bodies. On the ground of the seclusion of their women, the Sikhs would have objected strongly to the searching of their villages, and been supported by the authorities, police and Hindu-Sikh element of the army, and therefore operated from bases which were perfectly safe and sacrosanct.

The scared reaction to the air attack by the tiny Auster, armed only with one revolver and twelve rounds of ammunition, showed how valuable a few ground support aircraft would have been. The Akalis hesitated to attack without large concentrations, which could have been dispersed, at least by day, in open country offering little concealment from the air. The acute shortage of troops would have been greatly helped if a few support aircraft had been attached to the Boundary Force, even if used with strict restraint. The fiendish mass killing surely justified such a course.

A ghastly fate awaited abducted women, of whom only a small proportion were rescued and returned to their families. From the bodies found, most were brutally murdered when the Sikhs had no further use for them, as discovered by Clifford Williams. He reported, "I was driving down the Grand Trunk road between Jullundur and Ludhiana, when I came across the scene of a recent atrocity. By the side of the road were the naked mutilated bodies of about forty women, only one alive. The common mutilations were breasts cut off, and stomachs of pregnant women slit open with their unborn babies beside them. While I gazed at this gruesome sight, a woman without breasts painfully sat up, saw me and sank back to die, and as she did so pulled over a piece of clothing to hide her nakedness."

That such a macabre act had been committed beside the main highway shows that the evidence was meant to be seen, as part of a campaign of terror to drive out the Muslims. It was not an isolated case, as similar slaughters and mutilations of women were common, and appeared to be part of the Akali technique of war. In the Second World War appalling atrocities were committed, but these were not especially directed against women. No men have degraded themselves more than those in the Punjab who mutilated pregnant women.

The normal internal security rôle of the army was to support the civil power in maintaining law and order, but we faced a crisis in which the civil power was ineffective, law and order had completely broken down, and the reliability of the troops varied. Against those who failed in the army the usual disciplinary action could not be taken, for men would have turned against officers not of their own race or religion, or fought among themselves; Muslims against the rest.

In that tense and delicate situation Muslims had to be rescued, but it was impossible to save their homes and property, and by throwing those to the ravening wolves it helped to save lives. The key to the problem was to economise troops by concentrating the scattered victims where they could be protected. Food and water were the main essentials, especially the latter, as hardy Punjabis could starve for days, but in the heat of summer could not live long without water, which meant concentrating near wells.

At the beginning concentrations were made in and around the larger Muslim villages, which provided several wells and some stocks of food. However, that did not satisfy the Sikhs, who were determined to force the Muslims out of the last village, and so out of the East Punjab; a policy eventually forced on the Government. Those evacuated from villages under protection of the army were able to save their bullocks' carts, carrying a few possessions and above all, food, but those who had fled from attack before the arrival of troops had nothing, and suffered most deaths from starvation and exposure.

As more Muslims were ejected from their villages the evacuee camps expanded, and in many there were over 50,000. In the towns the same process of greater concentration continued, as keeps were reduced and became more crowded. While concentration helped the problem of protection, it made starvation more certain, for evacuees had to abandon stocks of food, which were immediately looted. The civil authorities very occasionally issued sacks of flour, but these were totally inadequate. While men and animals starved in the camps, the Muslims were forbidden to slaughter their bullocks by Hindu guards, so that often men and bullocks died together. A Hindu himself would rather die than eat beef, and therefore imposed his sacred prohibition on the Muslims.

The expression camp is misleading, for shelter from the elements did not exist. It meant no more than an open site with wells for drinking water, and perhaps water for animals in a river or stream. In drenching monsoon rain the site became a quagmire with the occupants soaked to the skin, and often ironically within sight of their empty houses.

The evacuees showed the greatest patience and fortitude in enduring hardship and starvation, failing only in the urgent need to organise sanitation. Though closely packed together, they continued the normal village practice of squatting in the fields. Because of lurking murderers they were afraid to venture far from the perimeter, and used the fringe of the camp as an open latrine, which soon became infested with disease-carrying flies. As dealing with excreta was beneath their status and dignity nothing could be done, and in due course dysentery and cholera became rife.

Many of the Muslims, including women and children, had severe wounds. The surgeons at the Military Hospital in Jullundur Cantonment dealt with as many cases as possible, but they were only a fraction of those needing attention. The Civil Hospital in Jullundur City was reserved mainly for Hindu and Sikh casualties arriving from Pakistan. An emergency hospital was improvised in barracks by a few Muslim military doctors, but with no trained nursing staff and few medical supplies. Patients were lying on the earthen floor almost touching each other, and cared for by relations or volunteers. Thousands did not reach even that makeshift hospital, and died in keeps and camps from septic wounds.

The first visitors from Delhi arrived in a Dakota aircraft on 26 August, and included Lady Mountbatten representing the Red Cross and St. John Ambulance Brigade, the Minister for Health, Rajkumari Amrit Kaur, and the Minister for Defence, Sidar Baldev Singh. The two ladies had come to assess the requirements for medical aid, and were tireless in visiting hospitals and nearby camps, where they spoke sympathetically to many. There followed a conference at the Circuit House near Jullundur City attended by the two Ministers, a few other politicians and civil officials. The only Britons present were Lady Mountbatten, her secretary Miss Muriel Watson and myself.

The conference was mainly about medical requirements. I was astonished at the exaggerated reports given about medical supplies allotted to the Muslims, and much indignation was shown when I proved that these were far from accurate. After her thorough inspection Lady Mountbatten had no illusions, but handled the meeting with great tact and ability, nobly supported by the Rajkumari, who showed more compassion for the plight of the Muslims than her male compatriots.

In the intense heat of August these two ladies had the courage to leave air-conditioned Delhi, and to endure the stench and horror of the evacuee camps and makeshift hospitals in Jullundur and elsewhere. On return they did not fail to act, and medical supplies began to arrive, but requirements were considerably beyond available resources, and during the crisis only a small number of the sick and injured could be given medical attention.

After the conference had dispersed I was returning to the Cantonment by the Grand Trunk road, which by-passes Jullundur City, when suddenly out to the left I spotted a large *jatha* advancing on the City, carrying the usual arms and long incendiary poles. The Muslims were then concentrated in certain areas or keeps, but only lightly guarded through lack of troops, and the Akalis were probably heading for a soft spot in the defences, or relying on friendly troops to look the other way. Luckily I was being followed by a jeep of the Brigade Defence Platoon with three Gurkhas and a Bren gun, who had been guarding the conference.

Ordering the Gurkhas into action I directed the gunner to fire one burst at the *jatha*, who immediately dropped out of sight in high crops. After an ominous pause a few Sikhs with firearms emerged, and began to skirmish towards us with all the skill of trained soldiers, alternately firing and rushing from cover to cover. The Gurkhas responded to each rush with a determined burst of fire, and soon brought the attack to a halt. If the Sikhs had tried to encircle us in the high crops it would have been awkward, but they began to slink away and I stopped the firing.

On withdrawing to our vehicles on the road, I discovered that we had had a small audience. Behind the cover of a hut were a few important-looking gentlemen wearing Gandhi caps, who had been at the Circuit House, and I wondered which side they had been backing. It was therefore a pleasant surprise when they congratulated us, and said that there would be complete chaos but for the army.

That incident showed that large armed *jathas* could be dispersed by a few resolute soldiers, who were prepared to fire. The Gurkhas showed no hesitation in acting, but unfortunately we had only one platoon of them, until 1/9th Gurkha Rifles joined us later. I was very surprised that a *jatha* should enter the City in broad daylight, which indicated that it had nothing to fear from the Hindu and Sikh troops there. A few Muslim troops would have made all the difference, but they had been diverted to the more urgent task of evacuating isolated villages.

Soon after joining the brigade I had my only contact with the local Akali leaders, when a dozen elderly Sikhs came to see me, who, from their dignified appearance and manner, were difficult to associate with the atrocities they were perpetrating. They said that the boundary award was unfair to the Sikhs, and there had been no proper consultations or plans made to meet its serious implications. The new boundary made an exchange of population inevitable, which should have been foreseen and organised to avoid bloodshed. It was clear that Sikhs could not live in Pakistan, where they were being butchered, looted and their women ravished, and therefore Muslims in the East Punjab must be expelled to make room for Sikhs from Pakistan.

As a soldier I told the Akalis that I was not authorised to

discuss politics, and advised them to see the Commissioner, or the Governor of the East Punjab, Sir Chandulal Trivedi. I explained that the army was trying to save lives on both sides of the border. For every Muslim they murdered a Sikh would be killed in Pakistan, and a political settlement was surely preferable to such insane killing of innocent people. Within a few days they were able to present their demands to the highest authority, Mr. Nehru, who had decided to visit the Punjab and see conditions for himself.

The Prime Minister spent a few hours at Jullundur, where he met the Akali leaders, Hindu politicians, local officials and Brigadier K. S. Thimayya, adviser to Major General Rees, Commander of the Punjab Boundary Force. As a result of his survey Mr. Nehru became convinced of the need to exchange threatened minorities with Pakistan, which was agreed by both Governments. So the Sikhs achieved their aim, but this did not end the slaughter, which continued unabated.

Although commanding at Jullundur I was not consulted by Mr. Nehru, as he preferred Indian advice, and therefore was unable to give him my appreciation of the local security situation, which differed from Thimayya's. Our difference was not surprising, as Thimayya was an ardent patriot with high ambitions for India, whereas I was a neutral charged with saving the lives of over a million Muslims, and our priorities differed.

Serious communal fighting in Jammu had already begun, and convinced Thimayya that a conflict was inevitable between India and Pakistan for possession of Jammu and Kashmir. He believed that reconstitution of the Indian Army should proceed without delay, so that it would be ready to take the field if called on. Thimayya's advice to Mr. Nehru, as confirmed in his biography by Humphrey Evans,* was:

(a) Abolish the joint headquarters of the Punjab Boundary Force under Major General Rees. Separate the troops of the force and place them under command of their own governments.

* *Thimayya of India: A Soldier's Life* by Humphrey Evans, Harcourt, Brace & Company, New York, 1960.

(*b*) Divide the old army between India and Pakistan, and reconstitute the new Indian Army as soon as possible.

(*c*) Hasten the relief of the remaining British officers.

There was no doubt that the replacement of neutral British officers, and the withdrawal of Muslim troops from India and Hindu-Sikh troops from Pakistan, would result in greater slaughter of the hapless evacuees. Therefore I could not support Thimayya, and, given the opportunity to meet Mr. Nehru, would have recommended the following measures, provided Pakistan agreed to reciprocate :

(*a*) In the border brigades not only suspend reconstitution during the migration of evacuees, but increase Muslim troops in the east and Hindu-Sikh troops in the west. 11th Brigade would be far more effective if one tank squadron and four companies of Muslims from Pakistan were exchanged for an equivalent number of Sikhs and border Hindus, who are too involved in the communal conflict to be reliable in saving Muslims. In Pakistan saving their own people they would be invaluable.

(*b*) The squadrons and companies so exchanged should each be commanded by a British officer, which will make them more acceptable across the border, and help co-operation with local security forces.

(*c*) Of the disbanded Muslim police many have crossed over to Pakistan, certainly those recruited from the West Punjab, but at least half have joined their families here in evacuee keeps and camps. They should be reinstated and placed under command of the army, and used to assist in defending keeps and camps. These police, and the troops exchanged under (*a*) above, would treble the Muslims in the security forces of the Doab.

(*d*) The time has come to do something about restoring law and order. By the exchange of minorities the Sikhs will achieve their aim of unity, and should therefore call off the killing. If, after fair warning, the Akali leaders refuse, they should be arrested by the Hindu-Sikh police supported by the army.

(e) To ensure closer co-ordination, the Hindu-Sikh police, who have lost direction and discipline, should be placed under command of the army.

These proposals, which I was unable to present to Mr. Nehru, do, I believe, give a fair and impartial assessment of the action needed at the time to stop the killing. However, Thimayya's recommendations had the full support of I.C.O.s, found favour with the Prime Minister, and were accepted by the Indian Government. Therefore the departure of British officers, and the movement of troops for reconstitution, were accelerated, thus hindering the rescue and protection of evacuees on both sides. Massacres continued, and no effective steps were taken by the Government to restore law and order, or to bring the Akali leaders to account. Thimayya's first recommendation was implemented immediately.

On 1 September, Headquarters Punjab Boundary Force with the unifying command of Major-General Rees came to an end, and the boundary troops were placed under separate headquarters and commanders. In Pakistan the troops came under Headquarters Lahore Area, first commanded by Major-General N. G. Gane, and then by Major-General B. W. Key. In India, Headquarters East Punjab Area were set up under Major-General Rees, soon replaced by Major-General Thimayya, recently promoted. Although co-operation between the commanders of the two sides remained good, that was not the same as immediate co-ordination by a joint commander in a critical and complex situation. Pete Rees had shown firmness and absolute impartiality, and I was sorry to see him go.

During the next few weeks there were several changes in the composition of the brigade, at a time when stability was desirable. As a step towards reconstitution 3rd (Para) Bn. 1st Punjab Regiment left to join the Pakistan Army, taking its two Muslim companies, and was replaced by 2nd Bn. Dogra Regiment who came from Pakistan to join the Indian Army. Because of their composition, both battalions would have been far more usefully employed if left where they were. 2nd Bn. Bihar Regiment left next to provide train and lorry escorts for refugees from Pakistan, and was replaced by 2nd Bn. Rajput Regiment.

As the Rajputs had two companies of Muslims and the Dogras none those changes in the brigade reduced the Muslim companies to five. The Communal War was intensifying, and looked like developing into a national conflict between India and Pakistan, with the result that Hindu-Sikh troops were becoming even more reluctant to save Muslims. I pointed out to higher command the great risk of withdrawing any more Muslim troops to speed reconstitution.

The migration of evacuees was about to begin, and without more troops it would have been impossible to guard keeps and camps, and provide escorts for numerous convoys. The brigade was therefore allotted another battalion, 1st Bn. 9th Gurkha Rifles. Commanded entirely by British officers the Gurkhas could always be relied on to act strongly, and were a welcome addition.

The brigade would have been greatly helped if left intact, not disrupted by reconstitution, and merely given the reinforcement of Gurkhas. Urgent rescue and protection work was interrupted by having to lose two of our original battalions. It took time to relieve, concentrate and move those battalions scattered in small detachments, and to acquaint the two new battalions with strange areas and fresh tasks. The effort and days wasted held up rescue operations and cost many lives.

CHAPTER VII

MIGRATION

When the Boundary Force was divided, new headquarters were set up in Delhi, called Delhi and East Punjab Command, under Lt.-General Sir Dudley Russell. In the Command were Delhi

Area and East Punjab Area, the two most concerned with the protection and evacuation of Muslims to Pakistan, and the reception of non-Muslims from that country.

East Punjab Area comprised two Sub-Areas, at Jullundur and Ambala, and four operational brigades: 123rd Infantry Brigade at Amritsar; 43rd Lorried Infantry Brigade at Ferozepore; 11th Infantry Brigade at Jullundur; 5th Infantry Brigade at Ludhiana. As trouble spread outwards from the new boundary, Ludhiana District became seriously affected, 11th Brigade had no reserves to deal with the situation, and so 5th Brigade took over that district about the middle of September.

Major General Rees stayed for a short while commanding the new East Punjab Area from Lahore, but towards the end of September headquarters moved to Jullundur, with Major-General Thimayya in command. Thus Rees had been responsible for the rescue and concentration of evacuees, and Thimayya became responsible for their evacuation. Lt.-Colonel P. S. Mitcheson was retained as chief staff officer (G.S.O.1) until the end of October, and played a major part in organising the headquarters at Jullundur.

The decision to exchange threatened minorities was received with relief, but unfortunately for the defenceless victims, political agreement between the two sides did not end murder, rape and loot. That could have been stopped if the security forces had been resolutely employed by the two Governments, but they preferred to devote their energies to a verbal and propaganda war against each other. Without clear direction from their new rulers, the I.C.O.s naturally failed to take strong action against their own people, and except for a handful of British officers exercising some degree of control, the losses would have been even more appalling.

That large *jathas* would scatter when firmly opposed by a few determined soldiers was proved time and again, as shown from an encounter by Major D. H. Donovan. He was second-in-command of 1/9th Gurkhas, and an experienced veteran, who had won a Military Cross in North Africa in 1943. His story is given in his own words.

"I was out looking at my area, preparing for the move of an evacuee column next day, with two jeeps each carrying a section of men with a Bren gun. When in a sunken track, looking at the countryside through field-glasses, we saw about two miles away a cloud of dust slowly approaching. After a short while it became clear that the cloud was caused by a large Sikh cavalry *jatha*, for I could see their spears and fluttering pennants as they jogged along. The sun was behind me, and it was about four o'clock in the afternoon.

"It seemed that the *jatha* was on its way to sack a Muslim village, or else to take up a position against my column next day. Either way I did not like it. So I sent one jeep forward about 500 yards, with instructions to open fire when I did from my command jeep. I let the Sikhs close to about 800 yards, and estimated their number at over 500. All were mounted, carrying spears, *kirpans* and shields, and the sight might have been straight out of the Arabian Nights.

"I opened fire with the Bren and rifles, and at the same time the other jeep party did the same out on a flank. Pandemonium set in among the Sikhs, who did not know which way to go. Then in absolute terror they turned and galloped off the way they had come, thinking perhaps that they had encountered a strong force. The *jatha* did not return, and next day, without a hitch, I escorted about 50,000 evacuees to the next staging camp, a distance of 25 miles."

The Sikhs had lost the opportunity of making fame by carrying out the last cavalry charge in history, probably to the relief of Denis Donovan and his little band of Gurkhas! His action was typical of British officers at the time, but unfortunately they had been reduced to only one or two in each battalion, except in the Gurkhas who had several.

Evacuation from the Doab was made difficult with only two bridges, one road and one rail, over the River Beas, midway between Jullundur and Amritsar. The latter town 16 miles from the new frontier at Atari, was the main Sikh stronghold, and constituted a dangerous bottle-neck for evacuee traffic. In South Kapurthala the Beas could be crossed by ferry within a day's march of the Pakistan border, and many Muslims went that way. However, the main evacuation routes were the Grand Trunk road and railway crossing the Beas by the two adjacent bridges. The main road was used intensively for foot and motor transport convoys of both refugees and evacuees, moving to and from the Doab and Ludhiana District. The railway carried those fleeing not only from the border districts, but from places far back in India and Pakistan.

Foot convoy was the normal method of clearing the rural camps, in which the bulk of the Muslim population had been concentrated. The bullock cart provided the best means of survival, as it carried food and the essentials of life. The bullocks or buffaloes were very weak from starvation, and where the roads had been damaged by the rains a whole family would be seen pushing their cart. Those without carts trudged along twelve abreast, with father, mother and the children carrying a few possessions, and in turn the baby.

As the hand-over point for our escorts to those of 123rd Brigade was the Beas bridge, a large staging camp was located a few miles short of the bridge to hold up to 50,000 evacuees. When 123rd Brigade, under Brigadier J. A. Salomons, could accept another convoy, it was there ready to cross the bridge, and the bridge camp was refilled from other staging camps. Those were located on all the roads radiating from Jullundur, and in turn were refilled from the static camps and a few Muslim villages still held and guarded.

Motor transport was provided by both sides for evacuees, and consisted mostly of army lorries with a soldier or two as escort in each vehicle. Motor convoys were used chiefly to clear the keeps in the towns, and few lorries could be spared for the rural camps. Occasionally trains were allotted, but with a shortage of rolling stock they were reserved mainly for the more distant places south of the Sutlej. All means of transport were organised by the Military Evacuation Officer (India), Major-General B. S. Chimni, and his counterpart in Pakistan.

A rail and motor transport transit camp to hold 80,000 was established on the fringe of Jullundur Cantonment, and included the large Muslim village of Garh Wahudan. Lieutenant Sardar Mohammad from the Dogra Centre was made responsible for that camp, which through his tireless efforts became well organised. Hundred of Muslims owed their lives to him, and I recommended him for an award to the Pakistan Government.

Protection on the move, whether by rail, motor transport or foot convoy, depended to a great extent on the individual soldier. With the acute shortage of troops, on convoy escort one soldier had to protect up to 25 bullock carts and 200 walkers. Lurking in the tall sugar cane near the road were the slash and grab parties, and unless the soldier was prepared to fire he was useless. In Pakistan a Hindu or Sikh guard did not hesitate to shoot, but in India only the Muslim was completely reliable.

The greatest density of traffic was along the Grand Trunk road between the Sutlej and Beas bridges, and Muslim troops were primarily used there, where they could protect most lives. On the march every day and on guard every night, in drenching monsoon rain, the men, who never complained. were sustained by the blessings of their own terrified people.

It was important to keep up the morale of soldiers whose families and homes had become threatened by partition, as they were the most disturbed element in the army. Units on both sides organised small parties to cross the border, and rescue families who were in danger. The commander was often a British officer, as his presence facilitated entry and movement, though it did not always ensure immunity from attack. Both in India and Pakistan some of the parties were ambushed and suffered losses. In 11th Brigade area the bravest of the rescues was carried out by Captain J. C. Ashton, whom I recommended for a well deserved gallantry award, details of which are given later.

In the communal conflict troops were naturally loyal to their own side, which created divisions and dangerous tensions in mixed units. Had the troops given way to their feelings and turned on each other, there would have been little hope for the evacuees, but fortunately the soldiers held together long enough to complete their life-saving task.

Brief accounts follow of the part taken by each unit during

both the rescue and evacuation phases; together these accounts describe the work carried out by 11th Brigade as a whole.

3rd Bn. Mahar Regiment, commanded by Lt.-Colonel Hari Singh, was the only battalion to enjoy continuity, for it was not interrupted in dealing with Hoshiarpur District, where it did splendid work. The many casualties occurring there were due mainly to the impossibility of covering the large area, and lack of police co-operation. Being low caste Hindus, the Mahars showed more tolerance towards the Muslims than high caste Hindu troops, who predominated. Also coming from Central India they were not emotionally involved in the Punjab, and therefore prepared to act. As a class only recently recruited they were anxious to prove themselves good soldiers by doing their duty, and succeeded, for the Muslims acclaimed them as their saviours.

3rd (Para) Bn. 1st Punjab Regiment, less its Sikhs and Rajputs, was the first battalion to leave for Pakistan under the plan to separate and reconstitute the two armies. On 7 September, its departure was a great loss. The battalion had a distinguished record with 4th and 10th Indian Divisions in the Second World War, beginning with the Battle of Sidi Barrani in 1940, and ending on the River Po in 1945.

In Jullundur District the 3/1st carried out continuous rescue operations, and was often in conflict with well armed *jathas* emerging from Kapurthala State, who endeavoured to obstruct and waylay traffic on the Grand Trunk road and railway north of the Sutlej, just as Sikhs from Patiala State were doing most effectively south of the river. The *jathas* had no success with the Punjabis and withdrew to look for easier game. There was an excellent understanding between the Muslims and non-Muslims in the battalion, of which valuable use was made by employing them in mixed parties, thus ensuring impartiality. By achieving that at such a time, their C.O. Major C. J. Boulter could not have made a greater contribution.

The second battalion to leave the brigade was 2nd Bn. Bihar Regiment, commanded by Lt.-Colonel Shivdarshan Singh Tur. After the ghastly massacre it was put into Jullundur City, with the task of concentrating and guarding the survivors in keeps. In the surrounding villages it carried out many rescues, and organised camps for the Muslims. The battalion then joined the Military Evacuation Organisation (India) to provide train and motor convoy escorts, and continued to do valuable work. At Gujranwala, across the border, in an attack on a train by swarms of Muslims, the Bihar escort fought valiantly and lost a fine officer, Captain Gurbachan Singh Grewal, and many men. For a brave action in which 1,200 evacuees were saved, several of the escort were decorated for gallantry.

In exchange for the 3/1st, 2nd Bn. Dogra Regiment came from Lahore, where it had greatly distinguished itself in saving Hindus and Sikhs from Muslim attacks, a task which much appealed to the men. Experience of atrocities in Lahore made the Dogras even more hostile to the Muslims, and it was hardly tactful to move them to Jullundur, where they were alloted to rescue work in the central area of the Doab.

As I had spent most of my service with the 2nd Dogras, and had reconstituted the battalion after the war, I knew most of the officers and men, and was delighted to see them, especially old friends such as the C.O. Lt.-Colonel J. N. Phelps, and the second-in-command Major E. C. Gleeson. Fortunately both remained during the critical period, and exercised a steadying influence. I appealed to the men to forget Lahore and to help in evacuating the Muslims, and they responded with traditional Dogra loyalty.

Under Lt.-Colonel N. C. Ghose and later Lt.-Colonel Ranbir Singh, 2nd Bn. Rajput Regiment was a wise choice for the task of saving Muslims. The two Muslim companies were a great asset, and as the two Hindu Rajput companies fortunately came from outside the Punjab, they were not personally involved in the local conflict. The battalion took over the northern area, which contained the last section of the Grand Trunk road up to the Beas, which, always packed with evacuees, was most vulnerable to attack.

During the rescue phase the battalion worked tirelessly in concentrating the Muslims. Later the Punjabi Mussalman com-

M

panies were used continuously as foot convoy escorts in most
exhausting conditions, yet were prepared to stay on their feet
until they dropped. No troops did more to save their own people.
For a time the Rajput companies were attached to the Military
Evacuation Organisation to escort Hindus and Sikhs from Pakistan, a task which they accepted with enthusiasm.

3rd Royal Bn. Frontier Force Regiment, commanded by
Lt.-Colonel J. L'A. Bell, was allotted to the Pakistan Army, but
remained until 15 November. With two Muslim companies the
battalion was invaluable, and during the rescue phase was mainly
employed in the southern area, including Ludhiana City. While
it was impossible to cover the rural area south of the Sutlej, a
massacre was prevented in Ludhiana City, such as occurred in
other towns. For that achievement James Bell had only half
his own battalion, and half 'B' Squadron C.I.H. under
Lieutenant Wajahat Husain, to whom he paid a high tribute for
courage.

About the middle of September, 3 R.F.F. Regiment was relieved south of the Sutlej by 5th Brigade under Brigadier N. J. B.
Stuart, and north of the river by 1/9th Gurkhas. During evacuation the former battalion was used to protect trains and the
main foot convoys. Train escorts in enclosed carriages had
proved easy to ambush, and on occasions the escort and all the
passengers had been killed. James Bell greatly improved train
protection, and discouraged attacks, by putting escorts on to
sand-bagged flat wagons, which were distributed along the train.
The battalion estimated that it had escorted about 250 trains
and 365,000 evacuees by foot convoy on their perilous journey.

On 13 October, 3 R.F.F. Regiment paraded before its Indian
and Pakistan companies separated. It was a moving occasion
to review together for the last time, Pathans from the Frontier
Province, and Mussalmans, Dogras and Sikhs from the Punjab,
representing some of the finest classes in the army, who for a
century had served happily together. For me the parade marked
the end of the old Indian Army, and of a great partnership. The
Dogras and Sikhs were replaced by two Punjabi Mussalman
companies, who increased the Muslims in the brigade to seven

companies; the need for Muslim troops to save their own people
was accepted at last, but two months too late.

1st Bn. 9th Gurkha Rifles took over a large and difficult
area in the south, served mostly by mud tracks, and flooded
in the monsoon. Commanded by Lt.-Colonel P. B. Keily, the
battalion worked hard and conscientiously in concentrating
evacuees in camps, and later in organising and protecting convoys. As citizens of Nepal, the Gurkhas were not involved in the
Communal War, and commanded entirely by British officers,
were reasonably impartial. Because the battalion always acted
strongly against the *jathas*, the officers became targets of the
Sikhs, and suffered two casualties. Major Bradford-Martin, who
had served with the battalion in the Desert, Italy and Greece,
was ambushed and killed. Captain David Forrer after a foray
had just given first aid to an injured Sikh, when he was
attacked from behind with a *kirpan* and severely wounded. His
life was saved by his Gurkha driver, Chandra Bahadur, who
drove off the attackers.

The battalion who caused me least concern was the 1/9th,
and so it came as a surprise when even the reliable Gurkhas added
to my many headaches. In October they asked to be relieved
of all duties for a few days to celebrate Dasehra, when their
arms were blessed by the Pandit, and they paid homage to
Durga, the Goddess of War and Victory, by sacrificing animals.
Because of the recent war they had been denied the festival for
several years, and were beginning to feel deprived of the protection of the Deity. Moreover they wished the celebration to
be a kind of last supper with their British officers after 130 years
of partnership. I pointed out to Subedar-Major Jai Bahadur
that 200,000 Muslim lives depended on the Gurkha guards, and
I had no reserves, but he was unmoved.

Faced with the problem of protecting the Muslims, Philip
Keily and I agreed that a short term risk was safer than upset-
ting the deep religious feelings of the Gurkhas, on whom so much
depended. It was finally settled that the battalion could concentrate for Dasehra provided skeleton guards were left behind,
which I would reinforce by denuding other areas. While guest

of honour during the decapitation of buffaloes and goats by one swipe of the *kukri*, with heads rolling in the dust, I felt uneasy about the gaps in the defences. However, the fine work of the Gurkhas after Dasehra convinced me that I had made the right decision.

'B' Squadron Central India Horse (Light Tanks), commanded by Major P. M. C. Hussey, was full of initiative and never failed to give a good account of itself. Troops were attached to battalions, and one troop allotted to work with the Kapurthala State Force. Using the Auster observation aircraft Peter Hussey devised a very effective method of spotting *jathas* moving to sack a village, and directing tanks to intercept them. On one occasion a surprised *jatha* arrived at a village to find the C.I.H. waiting in ambush. At first the *jathas* tended to move in large bodies of several thousands, but unnerved by these tactics broke up into smaller and less effective groups.

The Dogras and Jats of the C.I.H., though Hindus of the Punjab, were quite exceptional in being prepared to take strong action when murder was afoot. Two good reasons were, that the regiment had the highest traditions and discipline, and the squadron had a British commander. A further explanation is that the men were angered by the awful atrocities against women and children, which was not their idea of Communal War.

'C' Squadron 18th Cavalry (Heavy Tanks) under Captain Barkat Singh Bal, was also suballotted by troops to battalions, and used extensively for rescue and escort work. The frightening appearance and noise of the heavy tanks had a deterrent effect, and discouraged attackers. With their mobility and the fear they inspired tanks were economical in manpower, and we did not have enough. More Auster aircraft too would have helped in improving information, and directing tanks rapidly where most needed.

4th Field Company Engineers with Lieutenant J. L. Hindson and its Muslim composition was ideally suited for the task of saving Muslims, as the men were eager to respond, yet restrained from using excessive force by their British officer. The company took part in numerous rescue operations, and its engineering skill proved invaluable when roads were damaged by monsoon floods.

In the Doab the Muslims most threatened were those in the State of Kapurthala, where the security forces were predominantly Sikh. Fortunately I established a good understanding with the Sikh military commander Lt.-Colonel Jai Singh, and we mutually agreed that a tank troop of the C.I.H. would work with the state troops. Under an outstanding Dogra V.C.O., Jemadar Janak Singh I.D.S.M., their presence had a steadying influence on the Sikhs of the state security forces, and prevented the kind of anarchy that prevailed in the Sikh states south of the Sutlej. The tank troop also played a leading part in the evacuation of Muslims.

The action on 11 September is typical of the many timely rescues by Janak Singh and his troop of Dogras. Late in the afternoon an evacuee train crammed with Muslims and a State Force escort left Kapurthala. The tanks moved parallel to the train along a road as far as the state boundary, and then turned back. Soon after firing was heard and Janak Singh returned to find the front carriages derailed, and about two thousand Sikhs slaughtering the passengers. He immediately attacked and eventually drove off the Sikhs, but not before they had killed and wounded many Muslims and carried off two hundred women and girls.

Janak Singh was reinforced by Lieutenant Wajahat Husain and a few men of the C.I.H., the only troops available in Jullundur. Darkness was now approaching, and Wajahat disposed the combined party of about 30 to defend the train. With the cries of the wounded, and survivors looking for relations, all spent a very anxious night, but the Sikhs kept away.

At dawn a trail of women's shoes was discovered and followed to a copse about a mile away, which was littered with the mutilated bodies of about a hundred women, some still alive. Many babies had been murdered, but about twenty were crawling around looking for their mothers. During the night the women had been repeatedly raped and then slaughtered.

Hardly had the survivors been brought in, when another attack was launched by several thousand Akalis led by horsemen. A fierce battle developed before they were again driven off, pursued by the few tanks. That enabled steps to be taken to move on the train, which had been saved from a total massacre by the small party of the C.I.H.

Towards the end of September evacuation was in full swing, thousands had left in trains and lorries packed like sardines, and several foot convoys had crossed the Beas bridge, with another camped on the near side of the bridge ready to follow. The staging camp at the Bein stream, just east of Jullundur, was also crowded with evacuees. Then on 24 September, we were struck by a major disaster. Normally at this time the monsoon subsides, but it rained continuously for three days, with a record fall of 20 inches. The Beas widened from half a mile to ten. The Bein, normally a narrow stream, became half a mile across, and the railway bridge collapsed.

On visiting the Bein I found that the camp site had completely disappeared, and perched on tall trees in the racing water people were shouting for help. Steps were taken to rescue them and later David Jones visited the scene to find Sikh villagers helping with the operations. He asked why they were helping the Muslims when previously they had been trying to kill them, and was told that the floods were an act of God, which made a difference. Very grateful for their help, we hoped that the same spirit would be widespread, but met with disappointment.

It was estimated that 2,000 people and half the bullocks and carts had been lost at the Bein camp, for the sudden spate of water that came down from the hills at night had taken all by surprise. When the flood waters subsided the tragedy at the camp site was revealed. Dead bodies of about 500 people and 200 bullocks lay in the vicinity of the camp alone. While the Muslims were pathetically burying their dead, an old man, who had lost most of his family, said to me, "If this is Independence, bring back the Raj".

As it was not possible to get near the Beas bridges and camp during the flood, I flew over the area in the Auster, and beheld an awesome sight. The flat country was covered with water in which the villages appeared like islands. The luckier ones on high ground were just above water, but in many the flat roofs only were visible with the owners on top. It was a cruel fate that had brought such a terrible disaster on people already persecuted to the limit.

Considering the desperate plight of the survivors from the Beas bridge camp, it was thought that the Sikhs would refrain from attacks, but it was a vain hope. Protection became more difficult as people were scattered by the flood, and the Rajputs reported that, on the morning of 27 September, Sikhs had attacked evacuees near the Beas railway bridge, killed thirty and abducted ten girls. That was done when men, women and children were floundering in mud and water, having lost their carts, few possessions, food and probably members of the family. It is difficult to imagine greater cowardice and inhumanity; the 'Act of God' miracle had not worked at the Beas.

When the water receded sufficiently to make movement possible, I visited the Beas, where it was reported that about 5,000 evacuees and hundreds of bullocks and carts had been lost. The survivors were in a pitiful state, though still struggling to live and to reach Pakistan. Their leaders especially commended two people for heroism in saving life, Lieutenant John Hindson, Royal Engineers, and a local man. I asked to meet the latter, and was surprised when he turned out to be a Sikh, whom I congratulated and thanked. He was a fine type of simple peasant, who said that he did not approve of the cold-blooded killing of Muslims, especially women and children, and had done what he could to atone for the disgraceful deeds of the Sikhs. His atonement will always be remembered by those he saved.

It gave me great pleasure that the evacuees had praised John Hindson. Only a week previously I had congratulated him and eight men for driving off a horde of Sikhs attacking a train at night. He had worked for long hours in the water rescuing people until thoroughly exhausted, and developed pneumonia from which he died; a great loss to the dwindling group of British officers.

John had made the supreme sacrifice in giving his life for others, and was typical of the young British officers, who faithfully carried out their last duty in India. I strongly recommended him for a posthumous award. On returning to England I met his distressed parents, Colonel and Mrs. Hindson, to whom it was some consolation that their son had died a hero's death, but it would also have helped them if John's country had honoured his memory as he richly deserved.

The floods suspended all movement of evacuees by road or rail. Fortunately the Beas bridges were still standing, but the long high embankments leading to them had been breached in many places. Road and rail embankments and bridges had been damaged throughout the area. When the floods receded, 4th Field Company Engineers, the Public Works Department, and railway construction parties worked strenuously to restore communications.

During the floods I paid a visit to Hoshiarpur, and for transport used a three ton lorry because of its high clearance. Sections of the road were under water with the edges either side marked by posts. I was standing on the front seat with my head through the hatch in the roof to get a better view of the road and the country, when, traversing a stretch of water, I noticed sitting on a bank near the road a typical gang of *kirpan* slashers and grabbers. Suddenly the lorry dived into a hole where a culvert had been washed away, and with water rushing in the driver and I scrambled out and waded ashore. The highwaymen had deliberately given us no warning and enjoyed their laugh, but like spiders waiting for a fly to enter the web were disappointed, for obviously they were waiting for a lorry load of evacuees with their last possessions.

Having the roads and railway repaired became a matter of the greatest urgency, as evacuee casualties were increasing from starvation, disease and exposure. Bullocks on which so much depended were also becoming weak from starvation. A report from the Gurkhas at this time was typical of the situation in all camps. It stated that about 100 evacuees had died at Nakodar camp from exposure during the heavy rain. While the Muslims were dying in the rain-sodden fields without shelter their homes stood empty.

By the middle of October the roads and railway had been patched up, and it was possible to begin movement again. Every justifiable risk had to be taken, and convoys were provided with the minimum protection, so as to have the maximum number moving. It was a great relief to see carts, lorries and trains moving once more, and by the end of October splendid progress was being made, when suddenly the Akali leaders in Amritsar said that they would not allow any Muslim traffic through the town because of the slow evacuation from Pakistan. There was no truth in the allegation.

British officers, who served on both sides, considered that security arrangements were more effective in Pakistan than in India. In Pakistan more British officers were in command, at least half the troops were non-Muslim, and the army enjoyed better co-operation from the civil officials. The long hold-up in Amritsar had no counterpart in Pakistan. The men obstructing traffic were responsible for inhuman suffering and murder on a vast scale, and should have been confronted with tanks.

With the Muslim convoys halted, the roads were used mainly by Sikh bullock-cart convoys from Pakistan, which were moving to resettlement areas. Many had crossed the Sutlej to the south by the Ferozepore and Sulemanke bridges in the area of 43rd Brigade, commanded first by Brigadier John Keenan of the 1st Dogras, and then by Brigadier Sant Singh, who had been with me in the 6th Dogras, both old friends. The convoys then recrossed the Sutlej at Ludhiana to enter the Doab. Those I saw were from the Canal Colonies south-west of Lahore, and composed of tough Jat Sikhs, including many ex-soldiers.

The difference between the Sikh refugee convoys and the Muslim evacuee convoys was striking, for while the latter were in a pitiful state, the Sikhs appeared to be in excellent condition, with their carts full of healthy women and children, and drawn by fine fat bullocks. Many of the men were well mounted, carrying lances like a cavalry escort, while others marched strongly, armed with *kirpans*. As in battle to frighten their enemies their long beards were unrolled and flowing. I asked some of them if they had been attacked, and they replied that they had suffered a few casualties from rifle fire, but the Muslims had been too frightened to close in.

The determination of those Sikhs to defend themselves partly accounted for their survival in such good shape, but they were also helped by the availability of non-Muslim troops to protect them, and by not being disarmed and rightly permitted to defend themselves. All the refugees from Pakistan were not so fortunate, and those from remote areas suffered most. On the whole, however, refugees arriving from Pakistan were in much better condition than evacuees leaving the East Punjab, due mainly to a greater proportion of British officers being retained in Pakistan and able to help.

The incoming contingents fulfilled the aim of the Akali leaders to unite the Sikhs. I spoke to many of the refugees, and was impressed by their sturdy courage in adversity. They had lost everything, except what could be drawn through the dust by two bullocks, but they looked resolutely to the future, and soon settled down in the abandoned Muslim villages.

After days of wrangling in Amritsar, movement again began, and was helped by the urgency of resettling the incoming refugees, who were clamouring for food, accommodation and land. Only by getting rid of the Muslims could all resources be devoted to the refugees, especially food. The evacuees had never received more than occasional scanty rations, but even those became more difficult to provide as refugees streamed in.

Due to the war which had begun in Kashmir, there were also strong military reasons for clearing the evacuees. On 24 October, about 5,000 Pakistan irregulars, mostly frontier tribesmen, invaded Kashmir by the Jhelum River route. Two days later the Dogra Maharaja, Sir Hari Singh, acceded to India. That clearly brought to light a major flaw in the Indian Independence Act, for the future of four million people, three-quarters Muslim, was settled not by plebiscite or popular wish, but by the whim of one man, a Hindu.

Without delay on 27 October, India began to fly in a small force from Delhi to Srinagar, which arrived only just in time to prevent the Pakistanis from seizing, near Srinagar, the only airfield. The invaders were untrained, poorly equipped, and no match for the Indian regulars, who easily held them until more troops arrived, and eventually secured most of Jammu and Kashmir. As Jullundur became the forward base for those operations, it was essential to clear and improve road and rail communications, still only patched up after the floods, and impeded by evacuees. The end of migration would not only clear the roads, but also release protecting troops urgently needed for Kashmir.

Throughout November evacuation continued without interruption by foot convoy, motor transport and rail, and by the end of the month all Muslims had been cleared except about 50,000 in small isolated pockets in the Dogra foothills, who departed in December. That they had survived so long was due to the greater humanity of the Dogras.

Over a million Muslims were evacuated by 11th Brigade from the Doab, and many thousands from Ludhiana. At least 10 per cent had lost their lives by murder, disease, starvation, exposure and drowning in the floods. Most of the survivors who reached Pakistan were weak from malnutrition and ordeal, and many failed to live through the following winter. Muslim evacuees who had been Japanese prisoners of war, said that they had suffered far greater brutality at the hands of their own countrymen than from the Japanese.

The refugees who settled down best in their new countries were the peasants, who succeeded to the land left by the evacuees. But for millions of the displaced people miserable years lay ahead, as they wandered looking for jobs and homes. Thousands eventually migrated to Britain, which explains why so many of the immigrants from India and Pakistan have come from the Punjab.

Casualties of the brigade were, killed 3 officers and 7 other ranks, wounded 1 officer and 13 other ranks; the officers killed were 1 British, 1 Pakistani, and on escort duty in Pakistan 1 Indian. During the first two months after Independence the Brigade had an average strength of about 15 British officers, who, with the deaths of Mertyn Bradford-Martin and John Hindson, lost relatively more than the Muslims they were trying to save.

British officers had been steadily replaced, and by December few remained. Of the four British brigade commanders in the Area I was the last to depart. At a time when British officers with impartiality and mature experience could have saved countless lives, many were wasted in transit camps waiting for a ship to take them home. In their last rôle in India and Pakistan, those allowed to serve did not spare themselves in saving life, and lived up to the highest traditions of the British officer in the old Indian Army.

Elsa had stood up well to the ordeal, and insisted on staying with me until allotted a passage to England in s.s. *Empire Trooper*, at the beginning of December. We had continued to live at the Jubilee Hotel, at which the changes were in keeping with the times. In August most of the residents were British, but by December were almost entirely Indian, including some refugees from Pakistan. The Muslim owner and staff had fled to Pakistan, and a Hindu manager was doing his best to run the place with an untrained Hindu staff. The menus gradually changed to a variety of curries; and we longed for an English meal.

Elsa had to catch a train from Lahore to Karachi, and I escorted her across the new boundary. Before we left Captain West of the Dogra Centre asked me to give a lift to a young Muslim Pathan lady, whom he and his wife had been sheltering. She was a single woman from a high class family, who after Independence had endeavoured to return home to Pakistan by train, but on reaching Jullundur had been dragged out by Sikhs into the waiting room, and was being assaulted when rescued by troops.

A few months previously, between Jullundur and Lahore, the

same mixture of communities would have been seen anywhere along the road, but now a barrier divided a Muslim from a Hindu-Sikh world. We took the Pathan lady to the Lahore Civil Hospital, I put Elsa safely on the train, and decided on the return journey to liaise with Headquarters 123rd Brigade at Amritsar.

The Indian commander was away but I met his Brigade Major. He surprised me by asking whether 11th Brigade was ready to move in support of 123rd Brigade, if they had to cross the border in accordance with the emergency plan. He was equally astonished when I informed him that I had not been given any orders for such a plan. However, I had received orders to concentrate and prepare certain units for their move to Jammu and Kashmir, so that the brigade was in a fair state of readiness, and could have been used for an attack on Pakistan. There were two probable reasons why I had not been let into the secret of an emergency plan, except by accident : British officers were barred from taking part in a war between India and Pakistan; I was shortly due to leave.

Whether the emergency plan was a local precaution by the Area Commander, Major-General Thimayya, or whether ordered by Delhi, I did not discover, but it undoubtedly reflected the aggressive mood of all the senior Indian officers I met. Also judging by a letter from Mr. Nehru to Lord Mountbatten, the Governor General, the plan was in keeping with national policy. Following a temporary setback for Indian troops in Kashmir, which caused great concern, Mr. Nehru in his letter of 26 December 1947* stated that if necessary, India would not hesitate to march into West Pakistan to attack bases near the Kashmir border. Therefore he was prepared to invade deep into West Pakistan.

On 27 October, when India began to send regular troops to Kashmir, Pakistan was very tempted to do the same. She had the advantage of shorter and better road communications, and even two brigades at that early stage might have been ade-

* Reproduced in *The Great Divide* by H. V. Hodson, pp. 467–68, Hutchinson, London, 1969.

quate to secure the Kashmir Valley, and to block the only road from India by seizing the Banihal Pass. But such a move would have constituted an act of war as Kashmir had legally been made part of India by the accession of the ruling prince. The Supreme Commander, Field-Marshal Sir Claude Auchinleck, dissuaded Mr. Jinnah from taking so grave a risk. Any success in Kashmir, achieved by diverting forces from West Pakistan, would certainly have brought an attack by India against the West Punjab.

For any move against the West Punjab, Jullundur would have been the forward base, and therefore I had the opportunity of considering the prospects of such an invasion. The Indian Army had more than twice the numbers of the Pakistan Army, and could therefore concentrate in far greater strength. The many one-class regiments of the Indian Army had not been affected by reconstitution and were intact, such as the Gurkhas, Dogras and Mahars in 11th Brigade. But Muslim troops had all been in mixed regiments, and so the Pakistan Army, in process of being made up from fragments, was far behind the Indian Army in readiness.

By December, with migration completed and the troops concentrated, Thimayya's four infantry brigades and two armoured regiments were well placed to attack Lahore, only 19 miles across the border. In comparison only half as many troops were at hand to defend Lahore, even without diverting any to Kashmir, and moreover no defence plan had been prepared, or defences constructed. Following in the wake of an Indian invasion would have been hundreds of well organised Sikh *jathas*, eager to regain their lost lands, and to continue the massacres. I believe that Lahore, the capital of the West Punjab, would have been overwhelmed very quickly. If so, it was highly probable that the Afghans and Pathans would have invaded from the west.

If British advice had been ignored by Mr. Jinnah, Pakistan might never have become established, for popular opinion in India, fully supported by the army, was strongly opposed to partition. There was the risk that West Pakistan might have

been carved up between Afghanistan and the Pathans in the
west, and India in the east. Against impossible odds Pakistan
lost most of Jammu and Kashmir, but saved herself.

With the end of migration two major problems remained
in Jullundur; the resettlement of refugees, and the war in Kashmir. The civil administration dealt with the former, while the
army concentrated all its efforts in preparing for the latter. Mr.
Nehru, a Kashmiri Brahman, was determined to hold Kashmir,
and his enthusiasm spread to the army. Among Indian officers
Kashmir became a fanatical obsession, and nobody showed more
fervour than Thimayya, who later commanded the Indian
force there.

India continued to build up her forces in Jammu and Kashmir, first to consolidate her position, and then to extend her
area of control. The best veteran battalions were taken, and
from the brigade the Dogras, Gurkhas and Rajputs departed
amid much cheering. Their British officers had already been
replaced, and the new Indian Army faced its first campaign
without them. I was very impressed by the spirit of the men, for
although they had just endured four gruelling months, they did
not complain at the prospect of field service and more hardship; all hardy peasants, they were wonderful soldiers.

The clash between Muslim and non-Muslim troops, which
had been narrowly averted during the Communal War, was inevitable in Kashmir. Fighting which began between Indian regulars and Pakistani irregulars continued until the following
summer, when the Pakistan Army was sufficiently organised to
intervene and save what was left of Kashmir. Eventually a truce
was declared, and United Nations Observers accepted along a
ceasefire line, but subsequent negotiations failed to achieve a
settlement. In 1965 and 1971 India and Pakistan again fought
inconclusively for possession of Jammu and Kashmir, with the
result that no final boundary has been agreed, and a temporary
ceasefire line still separates the two armies.

By Christmas several units of the brigade had departed for
the war in Jammu and Kashmir, and new units were arriving
to take their place. As Jullundur had almost returned to normal,

David Jones and I decided to spend our last Christmas in India in the Dogra country. We reserved the resthouse at Gagret, north-east of Hoshiarpur, and set off to enjoy two peaceful days in the foothills.

That was the last view I had of the hamlets and pine clad hills of the people with whom I had served so happily. It brought back pleasant memories of the two summers before the war, when I had walked through much of the Dogra country, meeting old friends on the way. David, always cheerful and enthusiastic, made a good companion. Tessa, my yellow Labrador, showered affection on us both, and shared our meagre tit-bits. The old caretaker of the resthouse, cooking on a wood fire, did his best to serve us a Christmas dinner; Indian *murghi* (scraggy chicken).

There had been no social life in Jullundur since the Indepence celebrations, the Officers' Club had been quite dead, and therefore it was decided during Christmas week to resurrect the club and to hold a New Year's Eve dance. As Indian ladies had rarely been seen on the dance floor, and only two British wives remained, it was going to be interesting. Never before had so many Indian ladies in colourful saris been seen at the club, and what is more they took to the dance floor. Few of the men or women knew how to dance, but they shuffled round and thoroughly enjoyed themselves.

Apparently the men had said, "We are free of the British, Muslim *purdah* has ended, you are now emancipated, so show it". The girls obviously relished the idea and responded with enthusiasm. One of the healthy signs in India is the greater fredom of women, whereas in Muslim Pakistan the veil is dying a slow death.

On 31 December, I vacated command of 11th Brigade; David Jones and I were the last two British officers to leave that veteran brigade. He had supported me in a most difficult situation, helped the staff with his calm temperament, and was held in high regard by Indian officers and other ranks.

Lt.-Colonel Raja Naurang Singh and the officers of the Dogra Regimental Centre dined out the few remaining British officers of the regiment, which was greatly appreciated. For Lt.-Colonel Bold, Major Jones, Captains West and Wade, and myself it was a sad farewell to our old bachelor home, the mess, and for the last time we enjoyed the cherished tradition of pipers marching round the dining table against a background of the regimental colours unfurled across the wall.

Subedar-Major Sher Singh and the V.C.O.s entertained us at a traditional farewell teaparty. I was sorry to say good-bye to men with whom I had been happily associated for many years. Sher Singh and I had joined the regiment about the same time, and I had known him as a promising recruit, a N.C.O. and my Subedar-Major during the Burma campaign, in which he won the respect and affection of all. After the party had ended with speeches and presentations, we were garlanded and walked between two lines of Dogra soldiers, who had gathered to bid us farewell. For four months my work had been concerned with saving the lives of their new enemies, but their farewell showed that they bore no resentment. If fate had placed 11th Brigade across the River Ravi, they knew I should have been saving Dogras and not Muslims. And so I ended 29 years' Indian Army service, a sad milestone.

Next day I left Jullundur for Bombay to join the queue for a passage to England. I had last been on home leave in 1937, had not seen my mother or sister since, and so looked forward to a reunion with them and Elsa. At the end of the month I was allotted a passage, and glad to be off.

On the evening of 30 January 1948, several of us were sitting in the lounge of a troopship waiting to be towed from the berth, before turning towards England. There was a happy buzz of conversation at the prospect of seeing home, wives and families, when these pleasant thoughts were suddenly interrupted; the radio announced that Mahatma Gandhi had been assassinated. By then somewhat experienced in violent communal reactions, I said to my companions, "If it has been done by a Muslim, the Hindus will go mad, and we shall be lucky to sail tonight". But that final ghastly deed had been done by a Brahman, named Godse, and no disturbances delayed our departure.

N

On return to Britain I was not asked to make an official report on events in Jullundur. However, as British officers had been intimately involved in the rescue operations there, I felt an account should be placed on record, and sent a brief report to the Secretary of State, Commonwealth Relations.

On 10 October, in Jullundur, I had submitted a recommendation to Headquarters East Punjab Area for a posthumous award to Lieutenant Hindson, Royal Engineers, and on 24 October another recommendation for an award to Captain Ashton 3rd (Para) Bn. Rajput Regiment. I was not informed that they had been approved and forwarded. With the confused situation in India, I felt that the recommendations might have gone astray, and so I attached copies to my report to the Secretary of State, requesting that they be considered. I thought that was in order because both officers held the King's commission, and were more the concern of the British Government than of the new Indian Government. I was very disappointed that no awards were made.

Below are the acts of heroism of those young officers, as recorded by me at the time. Others were also worthy of recommendation, but I had selected the two most deserving.

*   *   *

"On the night of 20 September 1947, Lieutenant J. L. Hindson was in command of a detachment of 4 Field Company guarding Beas refugee camp. At 2000 hours heavy firing was heard from the direction of Beas railway station. With his small reserve of 8 men this officer moved towards the station, where a refugee train was being attacked by hundreds of Sikhs. He drove them off, and began to render first aid to several hundred wounded. After two hours' rescue work the train was able to leave. In the dark he then searched the station premises to find that 30 wounded had been left behind. He gave them first aid and protection until daylight, and then conveyed them to Lahore Hospital.

"On 27 September 1947, Lieutenant Hindson, returning

from Jullundur to Beas, arrived at Hamira to find high floods sweeping over the road. Many refugees were struggling in the water, while others, on top of bullock carts, up trees and on sand banks, were in danger of being cut off by the rapidly-rising water. From 1230 hours until dark at 1900 hours Lieutenant Hindson conducted rescue operations, and set a fine example by wading and swimming in the rushing torrent to stranded women and children, and carrying them to safety. His Company Commander arrived to find him in a very exhausted condition, and advised him to return to Jullundur, but this gallant officer continued for another half-hour in the dark until completely exhausted. By then he and his party had saved the lives of hundreds. As a result of continuous immersion in water, and physical strain, he contracted pneumonia and died three days later.

"On both the above occasions Lieutenant Hindson displayed the highest form of selfless courage in risking his life to save others."

*   *   *

"On 16 September 1947, Captain J. C. Ashton with two riflemen proceeded to village Sarjala in the very disturbed district of Jullundur to evacuate some Muslim families of his battalion. He met with much opposition from the villagers, who were very hostile to his proposal. After much argument he collected over 20 Muslims, mostly women and children, and proceeded to escort them to an evacuee camp at Bahram 4 miles away.

"Not far from the village the party was ambushed and fired on from high crops, and the two soldiers severely wounded. Jumping off the bonnet of the jeep on which he was sitting, Captain Ashton engaged the ambushers with his sten gun. It was later confirmed that they were five desperate men with rifles. After a fire fight, single-handed, he advanced and gradually forced them back until they disappeared.

"Captain Ashton then attended to the wounded men and carried them into the jeep, collected the scattered evacuees and continued the move. After half a mile the jeep became stuck in three feet of water, as the country was flooded with monsoon rain. With the assistance of villagers he extricated the vehicle, and finally brought the whole party back to safety. But for his gallantry the two soldiers undoubtedly would have been killed, and probably the others.

"Undaunted by his narrow escape Captain Ashton continued for three weeks to carry out hazardous rescue work, and saved hundreds of men, women and children connected with his battalion. In selfless gallantry this young officer lived up to the highest traditions of his race."

CHAPTER VIII

CONCLUSIONS

While there is general agreement that over ten million people migrated during the Communal War, it is less certain how many perished. The figure estimated from intelligence reports by Headquarters East Punjab Area was about one million. This I believe to be realistic, in keeping with reports received by Headquarters 11th Brigade, and with my own experience in the Jullundur Doab.

At the beginning deaths were mostly from violence, when whole villages and in towns whole streets were wiped out. The killing was reduced as the evacuees were concentrated and protected in camps and keeps, but deaths increased from starvation, privation and disease. Near the open camp sites the graves marked by mounds increased at an alarming rate. Pointing to their many graves the Muslims often said to me, "Sahib, if you do not get us out soon, none of us will be left". One million deaths is regarded as a conservative estimate by officers of the Boundary Force with whom I have been able to confer. Clearly

in the transfer of power security arrangements failed disgrace-
fully, but I believe this was not inevitable and could have been
avoided.

On 22 March 1947, Lord Mountbatten arrived in India to
effect the transfer of power by June 1948. He soon gained the
confidence of political leaders, and brought them together in
difficult and protracted negotiations. Because the Muslim League
insisted on partition, he failed to keep the sub-continent united,
but eventually persuaded all parties to agree to a plan, which
was accepted by the British Government. On 3 June, he broadcast to the Indian people that the country would be partitioned,
and given Independence on 15 August 1947.

In just over two months it was quite impossible to work out,
and implement, the countless details in the mammoth and complex task of dividing, and giving independence to, a slow-moving
country of 400 million, mostly illiterate people. The problem
was made more difficult by the time chosen, mid-summer, when
traditionally efficiency was at its lowest ebb, because of intense
tropical heat and monsoon rain. More time was particularly
needed to plan and prepare security arrangements in the danger
areas, and even two extra months would have made all the
difference.

In trying to carry out the plan for partition and Independence, by 15 August, inordinate haste created chaos. British
officials and police officers in key positions, and with a great
wealth of experience, were told to pack up and go. Muslim
officials were moving from India to Pakistan, and non-Muslims
in the opposite direction. In the Punjab no attempt was made to
retain a mixed police force, and on both sides of the border the
police became partisan and unreliable. In Jullundur, having got
rid of the Muslim police, the administration forbade the use
of Muslim troops in Jullundur City, where a massacre followed
almost immediately. The army's task was to support the administration and police, but these were no longer effective.

My views are naturally influenced by events in the Jullundur
Doab. Elsewhere there must have been slight variations, but the
general pattern was the same in all border districts, and on

both sides of the boundary. The dangers were obvious, but unfortunately the steps taken to meet them proved quite inadequate. In the situation which developed the main features were:

(a) Only the minorities were in danger, and when they became seriously threatened the new governments took no firm action to protect them.

(b) The civil officials and police, far from protecting the minorities, made them more vulnerable by disarming them of improvised weapons. They did not, however, disarm the attackers.

(c) Attacks were on a much larger scale than during previous communal riots. Security drill normally began with dire warnings to a mob to disperse, and if these were unheeded, minimum force was used on the written order of a magistrate. This procedure proved quite impracticable against mass attacks by thousands of armed men, and yet no firm Government directions were given to co-ordinate officials, police and troops against this greater threat.

(d) Despite large numbers, attackers were easily dispersed by a few resolute soldiers, but the only soldiers who could be trusted to show this resolution were British officers on both sides of the border, Muslims in the east, and non-Muslims in the west.

(e) The unsettled future of Kashmir added fuel to the fire.

For a century peace and security in the Punjab had depended on the British Army, and a nucleus of Britons in the Civil Service, Indian Army and Police. The sudden withdrawal of nearly all the British left a security vacuum, which was filled by men more in sympathy with the Communal War than its suppression. With the danger to minorities after the withdrawal of British troops, the old Indian Army and Police should have remained intact until the border crisis was over, instead of being disrupted by reconstitution and a change of officers.

When Independence Day was announced, I well remember assembling the V.C.O.s at the Regimental Centre, and explaining how the country would be partitioned when the Raj ended in two months' time. They expressed astonishment and the opinion that there would be serious disturbances and much bloodshed. While expecting freedom, they always thought the British would hand over in an orderly manner, rather than cut and run.

The bewilderment of sudden change was a powerful factor in the panic and hysteria that followed Independence. Confusion and instability were the direct result of everything happening at once, without adequate time for preparation. While there were good reasons for haste, there were equally strong grounds for cautiously phasing the transfer of rule, particularly with regard to security.

As described in the previous two chapters, the actual hand-over was divided into two phases; first, the hurried and incomplete preparations before Independence, and second, the transfer of rule on 15 August 1947 and the actions that followed. I believe that less panic and loss of life would have occurred if the operation had been divided into three phases as follows.

PHASE 1. PREPARATIONS

After 3 June 1947, the day Independence was announced:
Begin the withdrawal of British troops.

Before 15 August 1947:
Complete the replacement of all British civil officials and the exchange of those Muslim and non-Muslim officials who have opted to serve across the border.

Issue clear Government directions for the maintenance of law and order in the event of normal procedures breaking down.

Before 15 October 1947:
Civil Authorities, Police and Army prepare joint security plans according to Government directions.

Prepare plans for a Joint Defence Council to take over defence and internal security.

Boundary Commission completes its work including the settlement of the boundary in Jammu and Kashmir.

Settle the future of the minorities and prepare plans for voluntary migration.

PHASE 2. INDEPENDENCE

On 15 October 1947, Independence Day :
Announce the boundary settlement.

Hand over all authority separately to the two national Governments, except defence and internal security, which becomes a joint responsibility.

Joint Defence Council begins to operate.

Begin voluntary migration of minorities.

PHASE 3. DIVISION OF SECURITY

On 15 April 1948 :
Voluntary migration to be completed.

Each country becomes responsible for its own defence and security. End Joint Defence Council and joint command, and divide the security forces between the two countries under national command.

Withdraw British officers from the Army and the Police.

Let us now consider the above steps, particularly with regard to timing.

As there was no intention of using British troops for internal security, and as their withdrawal would take time, the sooner it began the better.

The replacement of British civil officials and the exchange of Muslim and non-Muslim officials was completed only just before 15 August. This was the earliest possible date for completion and so has been retained.

In the Doab the new Commissioner, D.I.G. Police and other senior officials took over their posts only a few days before Independence on 15 August, and when the storm broke were caught unprepared with no plans to deal with the situation, and with no influence over the local hotheads. They should have been given at least two months to become acquainted with strange areas, and to gain the confidence of local leaders, so that they could persuade them to exercise a restraining influence. As normal procedures for maintaining law and order were certain to fail in widespread communal war, the Government should have issued clear instructions for co-ordinating the Civil Authorities, Police and Army in joint plans, and allowed time for their preparation. These considerations meant that the earliest practical date for Independence was about 15 October.

An extra two months would have also made it possible for the Radcliffe Boundary Commission to continue its work, and to decide the Indo-West Pakistan boundary in Jammu and Kashmir. Once and for all this would have settled the future of Kashmir, which since partition has bedevilled relations between India and Pakistan, and despite three wars is still in dispute.

The Sikhs were as determined not to have a single Muslim in their country, as the Muslims were resolved not to have a single Sikh in theirs. To achieve their aim both were prepared to use terror and violence, but I believe they were not above accepting a reasonable settlement based on voluntary migration. A less hurried transfer of rule would have established the urgent need for migration, and given time to plan and carry it out with some degree of security. Four months have been suggested for discussions and planning, and six months for the movement of migrants lasting until 15 April 1948. The movement was actually carried out in three months, without preparation, and under the most brutal conditions.

With planned migration, arrangements could have been made to take movable property, and to exchange or sell non-movable property. Even at a loss few of the threatened people would have refused the opportunity to cross to safety. Such an operation cannot be carried out without much inhumanity and hardship, but this would have been trivial compared with what happened. Even if not entirely completed in six months, the problem would have been largely solved, and so would have removed the main cause of the Communal War.

The third phase is the most controversial as it suggests the retention of mixed security forces under united command for six months after Independence, until 15 April. Judging from events at the time such an arrangement would have been fully justified, as hasty division of the security forces and withdrawal of most of the British officers resulted in about one million deaths, thousands of women being abducted and savagely killed, and over ten millon people being subjected to untold suffering.

It would have greatly helped both governments if law and order had been maintained, while they were contending with the difficult task of setting up new administrations and of dealing with the migration of minorities. Peace and security could have been ensured only by temporarily retaining the mixed army and police with British officers under unified command. Faced with resolute and impartial security forces, the militant factions would not have got so completely out of hand.

Experience in 11th Brigade, and in the Army generally showed that British officers could have held mixed troops together for another six months; after all they had done so for two centuries.

The Indian Police had a fine record, but, after sudden reconstitution in the atmosphere of a communal war, they lost all sense of impartial duty. Their mixed composition and British officers should have been retained temporarily. Moreover the police would have been far more effective if placed under command of the army, and so closely co-ordinated with the troops.

A Supreme Commander, exercising united command both sides of the border, would have found it impossible to be subordinate to two governments giving contradictory orders. Therefore, to direct defence and internal security in both countries, a Joint Defence Council would have been necessary, with representatives from Britain, India and Pakistan. To ensure impartiality both the Chairman of the Council and the Supreme Commander would have had to be British. No one could have held these positions with greater respect and authority than, respectively, Lord (later Earl) Mountbatten and Field Marshal Sir Claude Auchinleck.

At the time a Joint Defence Council did exist, but with only limited functions. The Council suggested above would have been empowered to co-ordinate strong measures on both sides to save life, and to authorise the movement of troops where they would be most effective, such as more Muslims to the east and non-Muslims to the west. This arrangement was preferable to the inaction of two hostile governments, each waiting for the other to make the first move to stop the killing.

Finally, on the subject of security, we have the difficult question of whether aircraft should have been used to augment the totally inadequate number of troops. After flying for many hours in the small unarmed Auster aircraft and seeing marauding *jathas* marching to burn, murder and rape without mercy, slaughtering even small children, I have no doubt that air attack was justified. More often than not I was helpless to do anything against the *jathas* as the nearest troops were miles away.

The open country, providing little concealment from the air, was ideal for identifying and striking at roving armed bands, without unduly endangering others, and the deterrent effect would have been tremendous. The excuse for not using aircraft was the usual one, 'We cannot act unless the other side agrees to do the same'. The only answer was a Joint Defence Council and a Supreme Commander, who, respectively could make policy decisions and issue identical orders to both sides.

Undoubtedly some Indian and Pakistani politicians and army officers would have opposed temporary extension of united command on the grounds that it infringed sovereignty. But any sovereignty lost by either nation would have been more than balanced by the ability to help across the border its people in dire peril, through strong representation on the Joint Defence Council.

The more gradual transfer of rule in three phases as suggested would have been completed two months earlier than the date set by the British Government, which was June 1948. I am certain it would have saved hundreds of thousands of lives and appalling suffering brought about by unnecessary haste in abdicating responsibility. The Punjabis were among our most loyal friends in India, and it was very unfortunate that we failed to save them from a terrible tragedy. But for the small British rearguard of officers it would have been far worse.

The Governments of India and Pakistan were justly proud of the part their troops had taken in rescuing their own people across the border, and were generous in conferring awards for gallantry. In contrast the British Government was reluctant to recognise the valour of its own men, such as John Hindson and Jonathan Ashton. Perhaps it felt that the loss of a millon civilian lives was hardly an occasion for an honours list.

The soldiers in the Punjab, however, were paid a high tribute by their old commander, Field-Marshal Earl Wavell, a former Commander-in-Chief in India and Viceroy, who understood their difficult task. In his Foreword to *Fourth Indian Division*,* which includes the history of 11th Brigade, he wrote, 'The fame of this Division will surely go down as one of the greatest fighting formations in military history: to be spoken of with such as The Tenth Legion, The Light Division of the Peninsular War, Napoleon's Old Guard.

* * *

'It withstood even the supreme test of the period of communal troubles in the Punjab in 1947, where the Division strove impartially to prevent the massacres and to restore order. This was its last and its hardest service.'

* *Fourth Indian Division* by G. R. Stevens, McLaren & Son, London, 1948.

INDEX

A

Adams, Capt. W. H., 135
Afghan War, Third, 26, 29–32
Akalis, organisation of, 147; leaders and their aims, 167–8
Alden, Major H. W., 114
Amanullah Khan, Amir of Afghanistan, 26
Amrit Kaur, Rajkumari, Indian Minister of Health, 166
Anandpal, Raja, 89
Andrews, Lt.-Colonel H. A., 80
Army, 10th, 126
Army, 14th, 114, 130, 136
Ashton, Capt. J. C., 175, 194–6, 204
Auchinleck, Field-Marshal Sir Claude, 190, 203

B

Baldev Singh, Sirdar, Indian Minister of Defence, 166
Barstow, Major-General H., 67, 79
Beas, two vital bridges, 173–4; attack during floods, 183; attack on train, 194
Bell, Lt.-Colonel J. L'A, 178
Beynon, Major-General Sir William, 30
Bickford, Lt.-Colonel M. H., 77, 79
Bihar Regiment, 2nd Bn., 157, 176–7
Bold, Lt.-Colonel A. A., 193
Border, North-West Frontier, 37–9
Borrowman, Lt.-Colonel C. G., 19–20
Boulter, Major C. J., 176
Bradford-Martin, Major M. S., 160, 179, 188
Brigades, Indian Infantry, 5th, 172, 178; 8th, 115; 9th, 131; 11th, 149, 154–192, 204; 16th, 117; 27th, 129; 43rd, 172, 185; 45th, 30; 46th, 117; 49th, 138–9; 123rd, 131, 172, 174, 189; 161st, 131
Buddhist lamas, religious dance, 109

C

Carabiniers, 3rd (P.O.W. Dragoon Guards), 114
Cassino, Battle of, 128
Cavalry, 18th, 158, 180
Central India Horse, 158, 178, 180–2
Chandulal Trivedi, Sir, 168
Chappel, Major-General B. H., 128
Chaudri, S. R., 146
Chimni, Major-General B. S., 174
Churchill, Sir Winston, 61
Collingridge, Lt.-Colonel H. F., 33
Colson, Lt.-Colonel E. B., 116–7
Corps, 4th, 114, 131
Cowan, Major-General D. T., 130
Craddock, Squadron Sergeant-Major W. J. E., 114
Cropper, Lt.-Colonel R. A., 114
Cruddas, Capt. G. J., 80
Cunningham, Lt.-Colonel W. B., 67, 79

D

Dening, Brig. R., 122
Dewar, Capt. I. B. D., 80
Digby, Major T. A., 49, 51
Divisions, Indian, 4th, 121–2, 128, 149, 155, 157, 204; 5th, 114, 123, 130–40; 6th, 126–8; 8th, 128; 16th, 30; 17th, 117–8, 130–1, 135; 20th, 116, 133; 26th, 135
Dogra Regiment, 76–7, 113, 118, 125, 140
Dogra Battalions, 1st (P.W.O.), 113–4, 130, 133; 2nd (formerly 38th), 58–60, 66–88, 114–5, 127, 137, 140, 170, 177; 3rd, 115–6, 137, 140; 4th, 116–7, 133; 5th, 117–8, 136; 6th, 61–2, 124–6, 140; 7th, 118, 125, 140; 11th, 87, 120–4; M.G., 126–40
Dogra Regimental Centre, 77, 98, 119, 130, 140–1, 148–9, 154, 160, 192